SPEARHEAD

THE STONEWALL BRIGADE

◄SPEARHEAD►

THE STONEWALL BRIGADE

Steven M. Smith
and
Patrick Hook

ZENITH PRESS

Acknowledgments
Design: Compendium Design
Layout and editorial: Donald
  Sommerville
Maps: Mark Franklin
Reenactment photographs:
Bethanna and Joe Gibson would like to
thank the reenactors of the Stonewall
Brigade, whose dedication and
commitment to authenticity made their
photographs possible.

First published in 2008 by Zenith Press, an imprint of MBI Publishing
Company, 400 First Avenue North, Suite 300, Minneapolis, MN 55401 USA

Copyright © 2008 by Compendium Publishing Ltd, 43 Firth Street,
London W1D 4SA

Internet site information provided in the Reference section was correct when
provided by the author. The publisher can accept no responsibility for this
information becoming incorrect.

Zenith Press titles are also available at discounts in bulk quantity for
industrial or sales-promotional use. For details write to Special Sales Manager
at MBI Publishing Company, 400 First Avenue North, Suite 300,
Minneapolis, MN 55401 USA.

To find out more about our books, join us online at www.zenithpress.com.

ISBN-13: 978-0-7603-3050-0

Printed in Singapore

PAGE 2: This portrait of General Jackson,
with the Shenandoah Valley in the
background, was painted from an 1862
photograph taken in Winchester. Mary
Anna Jackson preferred that photograph
above all others taken of her husband.
*(Historic Lexington Foundation, Stonewall
Jackson House)*

PAGE 3: During the First Battle of Bull
Run, Jackson stood like a "stone wall"
with his brigade while appearing to be
seemingly indifferent to the bullets
whizzing about his ears.
(Sketch-National Archives)

CONTENTS

ORIGINS & HISTORY

First Roots

The legendary Stonewall Brigade had its earliest origins in the citizen militia units of Colonial Virginia. Beginning at Jamestown, the first English settlement on the continent, early settlers of the New World not only needed to be farmers and craftsmen but soldiers, to defend their fledgling communities against Indian tribes. Two bloody uprisings by the Powhatan tribe, in 1622 and 1644, reinforced this concept in Virginia as the colonists gradually spread inland.

As Virginia's population grew, jurisdiction over militias was taken over by counties, and one of the first known official units was the

Wherever Jackson's brigade went during the 1861–62 campaigns in the Shenandoah Valley, townsfolk paraded through the streets to the sound of the fife and drum, and impressionable young men filled the ranks of his five Virginia regiments. *(Century Magazine)*

Augusta County Regiment of Militia, formed in 1742 by Colonel James Patton. Later, this unit fought during the Seven Years War (the French and Indian War in America) when France allied itself with various tribes in an attempt to overthrow British rule in North America.

In July 1775, the Virginia House of Burgesses recruited regiments for the American Revolution, known as the Virginia State Line. The Virginian George Washington commanded all Continental forces, while local militias continued to be organized for home defense. By the 1800s Indians were no longer a threat east of the Appalachians; however, the War of 1812, fought for a time on Virginia soil, and the expeditionary Mexican War called forth additional martial talent from the Old Dominion. Another reason to keep local men in good practice of arms was the threat of slave rebellions, as the population of black chattel laborers in Virginia expanded to half a million, as opposed to just over a million whites, by the time of the Civil War. In 1831 a fearsome slave revolt led by Nat Turner in the south of the state reminded all citizens of the need to keep prepared.

For several decades there was peace in Virginia, though local men continued to be loosely organized, primarily getting together for monthly parties that combined talk, drinking, target practice and perhaps some rudimentary drill. But sectional tensions grew sharper during the 1850s, focused over the issue of slavery, and many communities began to take their martial capabilities more seriously, even in the pastoral Shenendoah Valley. This fertile section of the state, stretching northeast to the Potomac River, just west of Washington, DC, would supply nearly all the men of the Stonewall Brigade.

In October 1859, the abolitionist John Brown attempted to seize the U.S. arsenal at Harper's Ferry, on the Potomac at the mouth of the Valley. The locals immediately raised a militia unit from the county of Wythe, known as the Wythe Grays, which marched to the scene. After the fuss had died down the unit continued to meet, as did other militias, with more intense concentration than before. It soon became clear that Brown's rash action was just a foretaste of the greater conflict to come.

In December 1860, the state of South Carolina seceded from the Union, its example soon followed by other southern states, who joined together as a separate nation: the Confederate States of America. The primary issue was slavery, but the flashpoint had been the election to the presidency of Abraham Lincoln, of the new Republican Party. It was thought that the northern states were using their majority in population to enact anti-slavery and other policies that the southern states opposed.

Call to Arms

On the morning of April 12, 1861, Confederate batteries opened fire on the Federal garrison of Fort Sumter, South Carolina, an engagement

Born on January 21, 1824, and pictured here at age twenty-four, Thomas Jonathan Jackson, though poorly prepared for higher education, joined the U.S. Military Academy in 1842 and four years later graduated seventeenth in a class of fifty-nine. *(From G.F.R. Henderson)*

At a Confederate camp, an artilleryman poses beside his 6-pounder while scouts and sentinels remain alert in the background. *(Century Magazine)*

that signaled the start of the Civil War. Prior to this event, Virginia had not yet withdrawn from the United States; the open clash of arms, however, and the Federal government's vow to use force to put down the rebellion, caused a firestorm of sectional resentment. Less than a week later, Virginia announced that it, too, would secede from the Union. The people of Winchester in the Shenendoah responded by vigorously ringing their church bells. Elsewhere, couriers and telegrams passed on the dramatic news, which in many places resulted in cheering townsfolk massing in the streets. It was the trigger most of them had been waiting for, as the tension had been steadily building for years.

Shortly after the secession, Virginia's Governor John Letcher sent a telegram ordering local militias to seize the Federal arsenal at Harper's Ferry. It was an important military asset, not only for its valuable cache of weapons, but even more for its large quantity of arms-making machinery. Within two days, units from Charles Town and Winchester had seized the arsenal, which they found partly burned by its retreating Federal garrison, but they were still able to retrieve many guns, along with all the machinery.

In view of the Federals' vow to use force against the rebellion, Governor Letcher issued a call for recruits to "repel invasion and protect the citizens of the state in the present emergency."

Recruitment

The people of the Shenandoah Valley responded well to the sudden need to defend their region, and before long the numbers of men making their way to assembly points had swelled to a torrent—some walking, some sharing wagons, and others crowded onto the railroads. One newspaper printed a letter that stated: "We are in the midst of a great revolution; our people are united as one man, and are determined to maintain their rights at every sacrifice." As they made their way along the roads, the militiamen and volunteers were amazed at the scale of the goodwill and support of the general public. Complete strangers gave them food and shelter as well as clothes and, in one instance, a flag.

Crossing a stream on a low-water foot bridge, constructed by infantry. Taken at reenactment of the Battle of McDowell, fought in May 1862. *(Bethanna and Joe Gibson)*

In less than ten days, enough men had assembled in various small units to put together a brigade. These included the Augusta Rifles, Berkeley Border Guards, Emerald Guard, Montgomery Highlanders, Liberty Hall Volunteers, Mountain Guards, Rockbridge Rifles, Southern Guards, Staunton Artillery, Tenth Legion Minute Men, Virginia Hibernians, and the West Augusta Guards. (These colorful names would tend to disappear as the war increased in scale.) Between

Companies of the Stonewall Brigade

Company	Place of origin	Original CO
Second Regiment		
Co. A	Jefferson Guards, Jefferson Co.	John W. Rowan
Co. B	Hamtramck Guards, Shepardstown	Vincent M. Butler
Co. C	Nelson Rifles, Millwood	William Nelson
Co. D	Berkeley Border Guards, Berkeley	J. Q. A. Nadenbousch
Co. E	Hedgesville Blues, Martinsburg	Raleigh T. Colson
Co. F	Winchester Riflemen, Winchester	William L. Clark, Jr.
Co. G	Botts Greys, Charlestown	Lawson Botts
Co. H	Letcher Riflemen, Duffields community	James H. L. Hunter
Co. I	Clarke Rifles, Berryville	Strother H. Bowen
Co. K	Floyd Guards, Harper's Ferry	George W. Chambers
Fourth Regiment		
Co. A	Wythe Grays, Wytheville	William Terry
Co. B	Fort Lewis Volunteers, Big Spring area	David Edmondson
Co. C	Pulaski Guards, Pulaski Co.	James Walker
Co. D	Smythe Blues, Marion	Albert G. Pendleton
Co. E	Montgomery Highlanders, Blacksburg	Charles A. Ronald
Co. F	Grayson Daredevils, Elk Creek community	Peyton H. Hale
Co. G	Montgomery Fencibles, Montgomery Co.	Robert G. Terry
Co. H	Rockbridge Grays, Buffalo Forge & Lexington	
		James G. Updike
Co. I	Liberty Hall Volunteers, Lexington	James J. White
Co. K	Montgomery Mountain Boys, Montgomery Co.,	
		Robert G. Newlee
Fifth Regiment		
Co. A	Marion Rifles, Winchester	John H. S. Funk
Co. B	Rockbridge Rifles, Rockbridge Co.	Samuel H. Letcher
Co. C	Mountain Guard, Staunton	Richard G. Doyle
Co. D	Southern Guard, Staunton	Hazael J. Williams
Co. E	Augusta Grays, Greenville community	James W. Newton
Co. F	West View Infantry, Augusta Co.	St Francis C. Roberts
Co. G	Staunton Rifles, Staunton	Adam W. Harman
Co. H	Augusta Rifles, Augusta Co.	Absalom Koiner
Co. I	Ready Rifles, Sangerville community	Oswald F. Grimman
Co. K	Continental Morgan Guards, Frederick Co.	John Avis
Co. L	West Augusta Guards, Staunton	William S. H. Baylor

Colonel John Echols commanded the Stonewall Brigade's 27th Virginia. Wounded during the 1862 Kernstown fight, Echols recovered and eventually became a brigadier general in the Army of Northern Virginia. *(USAMHI)*

the units there was a wide variety of uniforms, though usually none at all. One company that stood out called itself the Continental Morgan Guards, its men wearing blue coats and tri-corner hats in exact imitation of George Washington's forces.

Company	Place of origin	Original CO

Twenty-Seventh Regiment

Co. A*	Allegheny Light Infantry, Covington	Thompson McAllister
Co. B	Virginia Hiberians, Alleghany Co.	Henry H. Robertson
Co. C	Allegheny Rifles, Clifton Forge	Lewis P. Holloway
Co. D	Monroe Guards, Monroe Co.	Hugh S. Tiffany
Co. E	Greenbrier Rifles, Lewisburg	Robert Dennis
Co. F	Greenbrier Sharpshooters, Greenbrier Co.	Samuel Brown
Co. G	Shriver Grays, Wheeling	Daniel M. Shriver
Co. H	Rockbridge Rifles, originally Co. B, 5th Regiment	
		Samuel H. Letcher.

* This company later transferred to the artillery, after which it was known as "Carpenter's Battery."

Thirty-Third Regiment

Co. A	Potomac Guards, Springfield, Hampshire Co.	
		Phillip T. Grace
Co. B	Tom's Brook Guard, Tom's Brook, Shenandoah Co.	
		Emanuel Crabill
Co. C	Tenth Legion Minute Men, Woodstock, Shenandoah Co.	
		John Gatewood
Co. D	Mountain Rangers, Winchester, Frederick Co.	
		F. W. M. Holliday
Co. E	Emerald Guard, New Market, Shenandoah Co.	
		Marion M. Sibert
Co. F	Independent (Hardy) Greys, Moorefield, Hardy Co.	
		Abraham Spengler
Co. G	Mount Jackson Rifles, Mount Jackson area, Shenandoah Co.	
		George W. Allen
Co. H	Page Grays, Luray, Page Co.	William D. Rippetoe
Co. I	Rockingham Confederates, Harrisonburg, Rockingham Co.	
		John R. Jones
Co. K	Shenandoah Sharpshooters, Shenanadoah Co.	
		David H. Walton

Source: *The National Archives Muster Rolls, Thirty-Third Virginia Infantry,* Lowell Reidenbaugh

Captain John D. Imboden organized the Staunton Artillery and in April 1861 brought the unit to Harper's Ferry. After First Bull Run, Imboden organized a cavalry command, the 1st Partisan Rangers, and assisted Jackson during the 1862 Valley campaign. Promoted to brigadier general in January 1863, Imboden continued to work with the Stonewall Brigade until stricken in 1864 with typhoid fever. *(USAMHI)*

A full brigade was officially formed on April 27, 1861, and at first was simply called the 1st Brigade, Virginia Volunteers. It would only take three months, however, before it acquired its more enduring name: the Stonewall Brigade.

Although the ranks of the new brigade were filled extremely quickly, the men were, for the most part, completely untrained. They came from a very wide variety of backgrounds and occupations, ranging in age from teenagers to old-timers (though young men were by far predominant). Most of them were either English or Scots-Irish by descent, with a good smattering of Irish, German and Swedish. Due to the local recruitment from the Shenendoah there was a widespread family element in the brigade, many brothers and cousins, or even fathers and sons, joining up together. One company in the 5th Virginia listed 18 different members of a family called Bell (only seven of whom survived the war). Of course, friends and neighbors also abounded within the ranks.

About a third of the men were farmers, the area being predominantly agricultural. Most had grown up familiar with firearms, either for defense or to provide meat for the table. But it has also been said that the Valley's volunteers made up the most highly educated brigade in the Civil War. This was due to the fact that the Shenendoah was prosperous, and many of the men had attended nearby Washington College, the Virginia Military Institute (VMI) in Lexington, or the University of Virginia in Charlottesville. General Joseph Johnston once commented that Stonewall Jackson was "most fortunate in commanding the flower of the Virginia troops."

The brigade was organized into the 2nd, 4th, 5th, 27th, and 33rd Virginia Infantry Regiments, along with the Rockbridge Artillery Battery. (The 1st Virginia Infantry had been put together in Richmond from existing state troops.) The regiments were further subdivided into 50 companies, though the 33rd Virginia was initially a company short. Civil War regiments were usually made up of ten companies of about

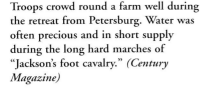

Troops crowd round a farm well during the retreat from Petersburg. Water was often precious and in short supply during the long hard marches of "Jackson's foot cavalry." *(Century Magazine)*

The fog of war – gunsmoke on the battlefield obscures attacking Union troops. Taken at a reenactment of the engagement at the Sunken Road, battlefield of Antietam. *(Bethanna and Joe Gibson)*

50 men, each of which was designated by a letter between A and K (J not used). A regiment would be commanded by a colonel and lieutenant colonel; companies by captains. A brigade, led by a brigadier general, was typically made up of four or five regiments, and three or four brigades would make up a division to be commanded by a major general.

The 1st Brigade was initially made part of the Virginia Provisional Army, before being reassigned to the Army of the Shenandoah on May 15, then to the Valley District in the fall, and finally to the Army of Northern Virginia in early 1862.

The individual regiments were largely made up of men from specific regions. The 2nd Virginia Infantry, for instance, was composed of volunteers from Jefferson, Clarke, Frederick and Berkeley Counties in the northern or "lower" Shenandoah Valley. (The Valley slopes down from south to north.) The men who made up the 4th Regiment were mostly from the "upper" Valley, whereas the 5th was composed of men from the militia units of Staunton and Augusta County. Those in the 27th were not strictly Valley people, being largely mountain men from southwestern Virginia. The 33rd was made up of volunteers from six counties, with the majority from Shenandoah County. One of its companies—Company E, known as the "Emerald Guard"—consisted mainly of Irish laborers.

During operations in the Shenandoah Valley, Jackson's men routinely cut Union telegraph lines to disrupt communications between Union forces in western Virginia and Washington. *(Century Magazine)*

The Rockbridge Artillery was initially formed from 70 recruits from Lexington who accepted an ex-West Pointer and church minister, William Nelson Pendleton, as their captain. The battery started out with two brass cannon from VMI, then another two gained from Richmond. The guns were christened Matthew, Mark, Luke and John.

Ready for War

With the creation of so many units, there was a serious need for field officers, a problem partly ameliorated in the 1st Brigade by the nearby presence of the VMI. Some of those chosen had previous military education or training, and a few had seen action in the Mexican War. Not all new officers had military experience, however, and some were simply community leaders or prominent businessmen. These included attorneys, mayors, state legislators and well-to-do farmers. The 33rd Regiment, for instance, had thirteen field officers: five had graduated from VMI, four had fought in the Mexican War or served as officers in militia units, and two had graduated from West Point.

The most important post of all, of course, was commander of the brigade, and Robert E. Lee, one of America's foremost soldiers, who at this stage was the commander of Virginia's troops, assigned the task to Colonel Thomas Jonathan Jackson.

Jackson had graduated from West Point in 1846 and served in the artillery during the Mexican War. Since 1851 he had taught military science as well as other subjects at VMI. Now he was faced with the task of turning over 2,500 raw recruits into an effective fighting force. He immediately began a severe training program. Despite, or perhaps because of, his strict discipline, the morale of the men was high, and their eagerness for battle was unexceeded.

Men of a Stonewall Brigade regiment examine a new battle flag. Taken at a reenactment of the Battle of Fredericksburg. *(Bethanna and Joe Gibson)*

IN ACTION

1861

As the summer of 1861 began, Jackson's 1st Brigade was part of Joseph E. Johnston's Army of the Shenendoah, some 11,000 strong, centered on Winchester. Pierre G. T. Beauregard commanded a larger Confederate force of some 21,000 based at Manassas, a key rail junction 25 miles from Washington, DC. Johnston had the tricky task of not only forestalling the larger Union army under Robert Patterson that was poised above him in Maryland, but maintaining the ability to reinforce Beauregard quickly should the main Union army advance from the capital. With Jackson's brigade as a covering force, assisted by J. E. B. ("Jeb") Stuart's cavalry, Johnston felt confident that Patterson could be handled, even as he looked over his shoulder for the main Union offensive to issue from Washington.

The view looking down on Harper's Ferry from Camp Hill during the spring of 1861 shows a peaceful town on the Potomac River surrounded by rivers and hills and served by the Baltimore and Ohio Railway. All that changed after Jackson arrived. *(Century Magazine)*

At the beginning of July, Patterson crossed the Potomac in strength and ventured into the Valley. Jackson marched forward to feel the enemy with his 5th Virginia, along with the Rockbridge Artillery and one of its "Gospel" guns. In the clash that followed, called the Battle of Hoke's Run (or Falling Waters), the 5th Virginia's 380 men vied with some 3,500 Union troops before prudently falling back on supporting regiments. By mid-morning the Federals had had enough while Jackson, having executed his orders to delay the enemy, returned to Johnston's main force.

Casualties were about 10 dead on each side with a number of wounded, and an entire Union cavalry company captured by Stuart's horsemen. At Hoke's Run Jackson's brigade experienced its first serious combat, though only the 5th Virginia and part of the 27th were involved. In mid-July Patterson sortied again across the Potomac but only milled around before deciding to return to Harper's Ferry. This worked perfectly for the Confederates because by then a much larger threat had emerged. Irvin McDowell with the main Federal army, 35,000 strong, had marched toward Manassas, and Johnston's troops from the Shenendoah needed to reinforce Beauregard for the first great battle of the war.

On July 18, Johnston ordered a forced march, led by Jackson's Brigade, to a station where the men boarded trains in one of the first strategic uses of railways in military history. They disembarked at

During July 1861, Jackson's brigade entrains on the Manassas Gap Railroad and speeds through the countryside on the way to the first major battle of the Civil War at Bull Run. *(Century Magazine)*

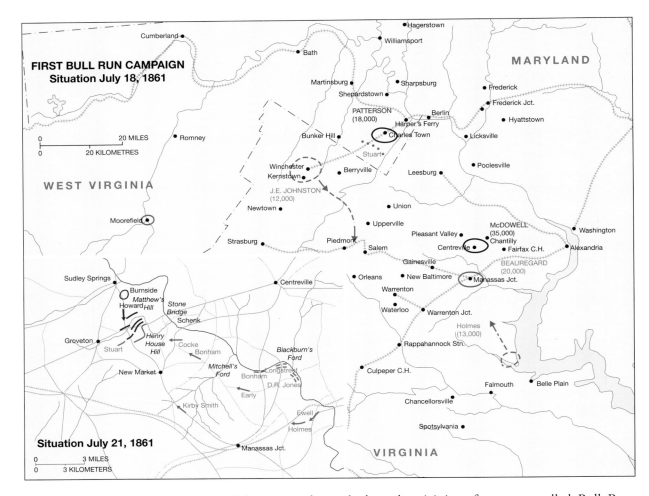

At First Bull Run, Joe Johnston rushed Jackson's brigade and other forces south to join Beauregard in the war's first strategic use of railways. They arrived just in time to halt McDowell's well-planned onslaught.

Manassas and marched to the vicinity of a stream called Bull Run. Johnston's rear troops continued coming off the cars even as the fighting raged.

The First Battle of Bull Run (or First Manassas), July 21, 1861

Like the Confederacy, the Union had been forced to mass forces on short notice, and therefore found itself with a similar army of amateurs. Lincoln's call for 75,000 90-day volunteers had been eagerly answered by the North, and the political pressure to crush the rebellion in its budding stages had been enormous. McDowell was not so confident in his undisciplined legions, but the gleeful enthusiasm with which the North supported an offensive forced his hand. In fact, thousands of civilians—politicians, picnickers and voyeurs—accompanied his army to witness the crushing of the rebellion.

Beauregard had massed his strength on his right, hoping to turn the Union army's flank once it approached over the direct route from Washington through Centreville. Jackson's brigade was placed in this sector. Once the battle opened, however, only long-range skirmishing

Confederate ladies of Manassas wait with their servants along the tracks of the railroad, listening intently as the artillery duel opens at First Bull Run. *(Battles and Leaders)*

across Bull Run took place before it was seen that McDowell had enacted a better plan. He had dispatched a heavy force to the north to cross the stream at Sudley Spring in order to smash in the barely protected Confederate left.

Jackson's Brigade suddenly received orders to march several miles to the north, where it deployed in line on the rear slope of a modest height called Henry House Hill. The 33rd Virginia under Colonel A.C. Cummings was the left-most formation, making it the left of the entire Confederate army. To the 33rd's right, in order, were the 2nd, 27th, 4th and 5th Virginia Infantry regiments. Artillery batteries under John Imboden and Hugh Stanard took position at Jackson's center. The clamor of battle grew to enormous volume in their front, and several men peeked across the hill to see other Confederate brigades fleeing in disorder, followed by what appeared to be solid masses of Federal troops.

Shortly after Jackson's men took up their positions, they came under intense fire, as the Union right had caved in the Confederate left, sweeping Rebel forces from Matthew's Hill and pursuing them across the fields. General Bernard Bee of South Carolina raced up to Jackson, who was calmly sitting his horse, and yelled, "General, they are beating us back!" Jackson replied, "Then, Sir, we will give them the bayonet."

Bee's South Carolina, Mississippi, and North Carolina troops had all but lost their cohesion when he rode back among them. Pointing toward the crest of the hill he shouted, "Look yonder—there stands Jackson like a stone wall! Rally behind the Virginians!"

Bee would be wounded only minutes later, dying the next day; his words would become immortal.

When Brigadier General Bernard E. Bee found his brigade under severe pressure on Henry House Hill during First Bull Run, he observed Jackson's brigade holding steady and spoke the words that immortalized the "Stonewall Brigade." *(USAMHI)*

Captain John Imboden and his battery accompanied Jackson's brigade to Bull Run and at full speed he pressed his field pieces into a supporting position near the Confederate position on Henry House Hill. *(Battles and Leaders)*

BATTERY, FORWARD!

THE CONFEDERATE SIDE AT BULL RUN.

IN THE THICK OF THE FIGHT.

Jackson rode along his lines and ordered his men to wait until the enemy were at thirty paces, then to fire and charge them with the bayonet. He told Colonel Cummings of the 33rd to keep an eye out for the Union artillery, and to keep his men lying low until the enemy advanced. Cummings did as he was told. However, when he saw a large Union battery unlimbering below him in position to enfilade his men, he realized that, if it was given time to continue its fire, his nervous men would break. Consequently, he ordered his men to charge the guns, and they did so with a fury that overran the battery. In spite of the 33rd subsequently being driven back up the hill, it was the turning point of the battle. Shortly afterward, Jackson's entire brigade poured over the hill, and the Union impetus was stopped. With Beauregard directing operations and Joe Johnston feeding more units into the crucial sector of the field, the battle was soon won.

The Federal retreat was at first merely hasty, but then became panicked when a cannon shot knocked out a wagon on a bridge, causing a massive pile-up. From that point it was every man for himself,

The Federal batteries of Captains James B. Ricketts and Robert D. Gardner played with effect on Henry House Hill until Jackson's 33rd Virginia charged across the field, opened a sweeping fire, and forced the enemy artillery to withdraw. *(Battles and Leaders)*

Order of Battle: First Battle of Bull Run

Army of the Shenandoah   ***BG Joseph E. Johnston, Commanding***

First Brigade	*BG Thomas J. Jackson*
2nd Virginia	*Col James W. Allen*
4th Virginia	*Col James F. Preston*
5th Virginia	*Col Kenton Harper*
27th Virginia	*Lt/Col John Echols*
33rd Virginia	*Col Arthur C. Cummings*
Rockbridge Artillery	*Cpt John P. Brockenbrough*
Second Brigade	*BG F. S. Bartow (killed)*
	Col Lucius J. Gartrell
7th Georgia	*Col Lucius J. Gartrell*
8th Georgia	*Lt/Col William M. Gardner (wounded)*
Wise Artillery	*Cpt E. G. Alburtis, Lt John Pelham*
Third Brigade	*BG B. E. Bee, Jr. (killed)*
	Col States Rights Gist
4th Alabama	*Col Egbert Jones (killed)*
2nd Mississippi	*Col William C. Falkner*
11th Mississippi (Cos. A & F)	*Lt/Col Philip F. Liddell*
6th North Carolina	*Colonel Charles F. Fisher (killed)*
Staunton Artillery	*Cpt John Imboden*
Fourth Brigade	*BG E. K Smith (wounded)*
	Col Arnold Elzey
1st Maryland Battalion	*Lt/Col George H. Steuart*
3rd Tennessee	*Col John C. Vaughn*
10th Virginia	*Col Simeon B. Gibbons*
13th Virginia	*Col A. P. Hill*
Culpeper Artillery	*Lt Robert F. Beckham*
Artillery	
Pendleton's Battery	*Cpt William N. Pendleton*
Thomas Artillery	*Cpt P. B. Stanard*
Cavalry	
1st Virginia	*Col J. E. B. Stuart*

General Pierre G. T. Beauregard, who initiated the Civil War on April 12, 1861, by firing on Fort Sumter, also commanded the Confederate line at First Bull Run, where the Stonewall Brigade arrived in time to change the tide of battle. (*Battles and Leaders*)

soldiers and picknickers alike. The Union army had degnerated into a disorganized mob that only stopped running when it had arrived back in Washington.

The battle had proved to be a severe testing ground for the troops on both sides. The Union forces left behind huge quantities of arms and

Brigadier General Bernard E. Bee, while organizing his troops behind the Robinson House, immortalized Jackson and his men by shouting, "There stands Jackson like a stone wall! Rally behind the Virginians!" *(Battles and Leaders)*

equipment, and lost nearly 2,900 men killed, wounded or captured. The Confederates suffered 1,982 casualties, but had the advantage of hanging on to their wounded. Jackson's brigade, with over 2,500 men on the field, suffered 111 dead and 373 wounded, the heaviest casualties of any brigade in the engagement.

After Bull Run (or Manassas), a wave of euphoria swept the South, as if their prior boast that any Southerner could whip three Yankees had been vindicated. In truth, McDowell had devised an excellent plan which, if not for the stalwart stand of the 1st Virginia Brigade, might have crushed the rebellion at its onset. As things stood, that Rebel formation would henceforth be known as the Stonewall Brigade, and its commander as Stonewall Jackson. In more ominous news for the South, however, the Union now realized it was in for a major war, and would begin massing its enormous strength accordingly.

After the battle, the brigade camped near Centreville while Jackson repeatedly put the men through drills and saw to their proper equipment. They were visited there by Governor Letcher who gave each regiment a Virginia State flag. It was around this time that the Rebels adopted the Confederate battle flag, based on the St. Andrew's Cross, because the Confederacy's official flag with a field of stars and horizontal bars had proven difficult to distinguish from the Union's "Stars and Stripes" on the battlefield.

In October the Confederates officially created the Department of Northern Virginia, and Jackson was promoted to major general to command one of its three districts: the Shenendoah Valley. On November 4, the brigade held a farewell parade for their General, who, though a man of few words, consented to give a speech. He said, in part:

> You have already gained a proud position in the history of this, our second War of Independence. I shall look with great anxiety to your future movements, and I trust whenever I shall hear of the First Brigade on the field of battle, it will be of still nobler deeds achieved and higher reputation won.

As it turned out, Jackson and his first command were not separated for long. When Jackson saw that a motley crew of half-armed militia were all he had to work with in the Valley, he requested his old brigade as reinforcements, along with William Loring's division of some 6,000 men. Command of what was now commonly called the Stonewall Brigade was given to Brigadier General Richard B. Garnett.

The Confederates continued to train and equip through the fall of 1861, seeing little action. In mid-December, perhaps just to exercise the men, Jackson marched north to destroy a dam across a shipping canal that led to Washington. Otherwise, the men adapted to camp life and its accompanying raft of diseases, particularly measles, while seeking furloughs to visit their homes.

1862

At 5:00 in the morning on New Year's Day, 1862, Jackson marched his troops from Winchester in a campaign to sweep Federal outposts northwest of the Valley in today's West Virginia. Though the march began in balmy weather, snow and icestorms soon came in, making the roads barely passable. The Confederates arrived at the town of Bath, only to find that the Union garrison had prudently evacuated. The unwieldly column then trudged north to fling some cannon shots at the town of Hancock, in Maryland across the Potomac.

The suffering Rebels then marched to the town of Romney, many of the men coughing along the way, scores dropping out with everything from frostbite to pneumonia. At one point when supply wagons finally caught up to the infantry, Garnett allowed the Stonewall Brigade to stop and cook rations. Jackson rode up and said there was no time to stop, but Garnett replied that it was impossible for the men to continue without eating. "I never found anything impossible with this brigade," Jackson grumbled before riding away.

Romney, too, turned out to be evacuated by Federal forces, though the hungry Confederates were able to find some abandoned supplies. Jackson left Loring's division as a garrison for the town and then returned to the more accommodating Shenendoah Valley with the Stonewall Brigade. He claimed the 23-day campaign as a success,

During the failed Romney campaign in January 1862, a Confederate sentinel from Jackson's brigade tries to keep warm as a winter blizzard accompanied by subzero temperatures blows through camp. *(Century Magazine)*

reporting that he had only suffered four dead and 28 wounded. What he failed to mention was that 1,200 of his men were now in hospitals due to the freezing conditions, and that hundreds of others had deserted on the march.

It is worth mentioning that the Stonewall Brigade, for all its renown, consistently had one of the worst desertion rates of any formation in the Civil War. This was primarily because the brigade was raised in and around the Shenendoah Valley, so that nearly every man had parents, relatives or friends near at hand to whose homes they could take respite. Carolina, Georgia, or Mississippi troops dispatched to Virginia did not have such quick recourse to succor, and could not go back and forth from the army so easily.

Jackson's force went into winter quarters around Winchester where it recuperated and found its ranks enhanced considerably. Due to a system of bounties and furloughs, nearly all the men re-enlisted, and local militia units were incorporated into the army. With the most impact of all, the Confederate government planned to begin conscripting all able-bodied men between the ages of 18 and 35, but in the meantime all who volunteered could join which regiments they wished. The Stonewall Brigade, already famous and consisting of local men from the Valley, found itself with a huge influx of recruits. By the time the draft commenced on April 16 the brigade rolls listed over 3,600 men, though this number was never sustained.

The Federals, too, had spent the past six months enlarging and training their forces, the principal element of which was the Army of the Potomac, well over 100,000 strong, led by George B. McClellan. In March, McClellan demonstrated toward Centreville, even as unmistakable signs emerged that his true plan was a grand amphibious movement to the Virginia Peninsula to assault Richmond from the east. General Johnston pulled the main Confederate army behind the Rappahannock River, the better to resist an overland thrust or to move to the defense of the capital if necessary. Another Federal force under John C. Fremont, some 15,000 strong, was in the Allegheny Mountains west of the Shenendoah, while still another Federal corps of about 20,000 men under Nathaniel Banks lay around Harper's Ferry to the Valley's north.

Stonewall Jackson only had some 3,600 infantry, consisting of his old brigade and two smaller ones, plus 600 cavalry under the dashing Turner Ashby; but his orders were to tie down the Federal forces in the Valley so they would be unable to join McClellan. When Banks advanced south from the Potomac in early March, Jackson fell back before him. He evacuated Winchester on the 11th, and then retreated another 40 miles, as Ashby vied with advance Union cavalry in what would become almost daily duels.

Jedediah Hotchkiss went to work as a cartographer for Jackson on March 26, 1862, when the general asked him to make a map of the Shenandoah Valley. This began an association that made Hotchkiss the foremost mapmaker of the war. (*John Wayland's* Stonewall Jackson's Way)

Banks began to suspect that he was unopposed in the Shenendoah, and proposed that part of his corps be allowed to join McClellan. In mid-March the Confederate forces of the Valley District became part of the newly named Army of Northern Virginia, and Joe Johnston suggested to Jackson that he stay closer to Banks in order to keep him occupied. This was all the impetus Jackson needed for a fight. On March 22, he marched his force 28 miles back down the Valley. After a few hours late-night sleep he drove his men for 15 more miles, arriving in the afternoon near enemy positions at Kernstown, three miles south of Winchester.

The Battle of Kernstown, March 23, 1862

At first Jackson was inclined to let his men rest and allow time for stragglers to catch up, but he was informed that there were only four Federal regiments in Kernstown. Rather than wait for the enemy to be reinforced, Jackson decided to strike immediately.

Positioning his artillery and cavalry astride the Valley turnpike, Jackson dispatched the bulk of his force to a ridge on his left to flank the enemy position. The Stonewall Brigade, less the 5th Virginia held in reserve, manned the center of the Confederate line. An early highpoint of the battle occurred when the 37th Virginia and a Federal regiment staged a footrace for a stone fence that lay parallel and midway between them.

"It was 'nip and tuck' which would reach it first," said an observing Stonewaller, "but the 37th Virginia got there first, and, kneeling down, poured a deadly volley into the other at close quarters and nearly annihilated it. Such would have been their fate if the Federals had gotten there first."

At the Battle of Kernstown on March 23, 1861, a Confederate private ducks behind a tree stump to reload his musket before rejoining his company. (*Century Magazine*)

Order of Battle: First Battle of Kernstown

Valley District   **MG Thomas J. Jackson**

Stonewall Brigade   *BG Richard B. Garnett*
     2nd Virginia, 4th Virginia, 5th Virginia, 27th Virginia,
     33rd Virginia, Rockbridge Artillery, West Augusta (Virginia) Artillery,
     Carpenter's Virginia Battery

Burks' Brigade   *Colonel Jesse S. Burks*
     21st Virginia, 42nd Virginia, 48th Virginia *(not engaged)*,
     1st Virginia (Irish) Battalion, Pleasant's (Virginia) Battery *(not engaged)*

Fulkerson's Brigade   *Colonel Samuel V. Fulkerson*
     23rd Virginia, 37th Virginia, Danville Artillery *(not engaged)*

Cavalry   *Colonel Turner Ashby*
     7th Virginia, Chew's (Virginia) Battery, Horse Artillery

The Stonewall Brigade advanced on the ridge and stood under a constant hail of shells and bullets as the Federal forces in their front grew ever larger. It turned out that the Confederates had not taken on a mere four regiments but Union General James Shields' entire division of about 8,000 men. Further, Jackson, directing the artillery on the right, was failing to keep the main enemy force pinned down. Up on the ridge, Richard Garnett began to receive reports from his regimental commanders that the men were running out of ammunition. The Federals were advancing on both flanks and would soon have the brigade surrounded.

Jackson started reinforcements to the ridge, but Garnett felt he couldn't hang on a moment longer. He ordered a withdrawal, instructing the 5th Virginia to stay in the rear to form a line to protect the retreat. Jackson rode up and was furious to see his battle line melting away. He ordered a drummer boy to "Beat the rally!" but the retreat only grew more chaotic as exultant Federals poured over the ridge. The 5th and 42nd Virginia were able to stand fast to stop the pursuit, but most of the army didn't stop till it had made another five miles down the turnpike.

Of just over 1,400 men engaged, the Stonewall Brigade lost 343, and Jackson's entire force about 700. Due to straggling on the forced march, the Confederates had put fewer than 3,000 men in the fight. The Federals counted their losses at 584. A few days later Jackson put Garnett under arrest for retreating without orders. Nearly every officer in the brigade rose to defend their brigadier, and the court martial never took place. Garnett was later given a brigade in George Pickett's division, and died at the head of his troops at Gettysburg.

Kernstown was Stonewall Jackson's only battlefield defeat (even if he never admitted it), but ironically it turned into a strategic victory for the Confederacy. The ferocity of the battle alarmed Lincoln and his advisers, prompting them temporarily to halt overland reinforcements to McClellan. Not only was Banks' corps ordered to stay in the Valley, but a larger one under McDowell was held in place near Fredericksburg for a potential defense of Washington. Meantime, Fremont was ordered to advance on the Valley from the west in order to eradicate the threat that Stonewall had presented.

By April, McClellan's move to the Peninsula had become obvious, and Johnston marched the Army of Northern Virginia to confront the Army of the Potomac. It was essential that the 60,000 Union troops operating elsewhere in Virginia be prevented from joining McClellan, which meant that Jackson needed to be reinforced. In addition to his existing men, he was given Richard S. Ewell's division of 8,000 and Edward Johnson's force of nearly 3,000 that was posted in the Alleghenies.

On March 23, 1862, Brigadier General James Shields bested Jackson's brigade at Kernstown, but during all the subsequent battles in the Shenandoah Valley, Jackson out-maneuvered Shields and every other Union general. *(USAMHI)*

The Stonewall Brigade, upset enough at Garnett's arrest, was disturbed even further when Charles S. Winder, a West Pointer from Maryland, was put in charge. The Valley men had not yet been commanded by an outsider, and felt that one of their own regimental officers deserved the honor. Winder was also an imperious, spit-and-polish type who demanded strict discipline. Eventually it would become clear that he was an excellent fighter, though not all the men would warm to him.

At the end of April, Richard Taylor, who commanded a Louisiana brigade in Ewell's division, met Jackson for the first time and recorded his initial thoughts:

> He then by no means held the place in public estimation which he subsequently attained . . . The winter march on Romney had resulted in little except to freeze and discontent the troops; which discontent was shared and expressed by the authorites at Richmond . . . At Kernstown . . . he was roughly handled by the Federal General Shields, and only saved from serious disaster by the failure of that officer to push his advantage.

It had to some degree been a winter of discontent; however with the warmth of spring, plus significant reinforcements, the fame of Jackson and the Stonewall Brigade would soon reach new heights.

The Valley Campaign
The Battle of McDowell, May 8, 1862

In early May, Nathaniel Banks headed up the Valley with a force of 19,000 men, while Fremont dispatched part of his force under Robert Milroy toward the upper Valley from the west. Jackson camped at a place called Conrad's Store, at the south end of Massanutten Mountain, a huge ridge that split the Shenendoah into two parallel valleys for 45 miles. There was only one crossing of the massif, between New Market and Luray, and the ridge also split the Shenendoah River into two streams called the North Fork and South Fork.

When Ewell arrived to join Jackson at Conrad's Store, all he found was an empty campground and vague instructions to attack Banks if the Federals continued to move south. Jackson had meanwhile marched over the Blue Ridge Mountains to the east, as if he were retreating or moving to reinforce the army at Richmond. To the delight of the Stonewall Brigade, however, they were put aboard cars of the Virginia Central Railroad, to travel by rail back to the upper Valley at Staunton.

Jackson's men then joined Ed Johnson's command, which was confronting Milroy in the Allegheny foothills. The Federals were reinforced to about 6,000 men. The Stonewall Brigade had yet to arrive on the field on May 8 when the Federals attacked Johnson's positions

Union General Robert Milroy had the misfortune of being drubbed by the Comfederates at McDowell on May 8, 1862, and routed again on June 12, 1863, when the 5th Virginia scaled a range of hills overlooking Winchester and opened the way for Ewell's II Corps to flush the Federals out of the Valley. *(USAMHI)*

on the heights. In order to reach the battle from Staunton, the Stonewall Brigade made a 36-mile march, the first 20 with full equipment. Jackson then ordered them to leave their packs and continue at the double-quick.

The Federals attacked because they thought the Confederates were about to place batteries on a commanding height; in point of fact, due to the terrain, the battle was fought almost without artillery. After the Union troops were repulsed on the hillsides they withdrew to McDowell, lighting campfires to disguise their retreat. The next day the Stonewall Brigade pursued the column, which was falling back toward other elements of Fremont's army. The battle had cost each side several hundred men, with the more important result that Fremont had been temporarily removed from the campaign. Now Jackson could concentrate on Banks.

The Battles of Front Royal and First Winchester, May 23, 1862

After weeks of lying relatively undisturbed in the lower Valley, Federal General Banks had grown anxious to join the momentous campaign then unfolding before Richmond. Jackson's feint east of the Blue Ridge had fooled him into thinking that Confederate forces were vacating the Shenendoah. Instead of transferring Banks, however, the authorities in Washington simply stripped him of his division under Shields, leaving the civilian-soldier with only 10,000 men. And now Jackson had united his division with Ewell's and Ed Johnson's for a total of 17,000, and the entire force was moving down the Valley.

Banks deployed about 7,500 of his men near Strasburg, at the northwest shoulder of Massanutten facing up the Valley Pike, upon which he expected Jackson to march. He placed 1,000 more at Front Royal at the mountain's northeast shoulder, and kept the remainder of his force, some 1,500, around Winchester to guard his main supply depot and communications.

Jackson began marching straight down the Shenendoah Valley toward Banks' prepared positions at Strasburg. At the town of New Market, though, he suddenly turned east over the pass that bisected Massanutten. It was as if he had suddenly disappeared from Banks' front. In the narrower Luray Valley he joined up with the remainder of Ewell's division and continued his march north, now screened by the mountain, his entire army approaching the small Union garrison at Front Royal.

As usual, Jackson went into battle without waiting for his stragglers to catch up, not wishing to squander the element of surprise. The defenders of Front Royal pulled back to high ground and put up a good fight, assisted by two 10-pounder Parrott guns, but Confederate formations kept pouring onto the field. Jackson's own artillery came up

Colonel William B. Taliaferro commanded the 23rd Virginia in a manner that never completely satisfied Jackson until the 1862 Valley campaign. Promoted to brigadier general, Taliaferro fought well and distinguished himself at Port Republic, Cedar Mountain, Brawner's Farm, and Fredericksburg. *(USAMHI)*

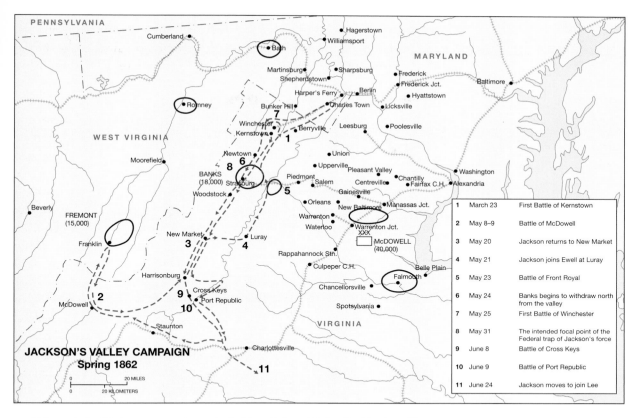

1	March 23	First Battle of Kernstown
2	May 8–9	Battle of McDowell
3	May 20	Jackson returns to New Market
4	May 21	Jackson joins Ewell at Luray
5	May 23	Battle of Front Royal
6	May 24	Banks begins to withdraw north from the valley
7	May 25	First Battle of Winchester
8	May 31	The intended focal point of the Federal trap of Jackson's force
9	June 8	Battle of Cross Keys
10	June 9	Battle of Port Republic
11	June 24	Jackson moves to join Lee

JACKSON'S VALLEY CAMPAIGN
Spring 1862

and blasted the Union troops, bravely led by Colonel John R. Kenly, off their hill. The defenders scrambled across the Shenendoah River and tried to set fire to the bridge behind them, but Jackson's men were too close and put out the flames. Ashby's cavalry was able to cross at a nearby ford and went slashing through the retreating ranks. In the end, Kenly's force was all but obliterated, he himself was wounded, and some 700 of his men were taken prisoner. The Confederates only suffered a few dozen casualties.

Banks was strangely obstinate after hearing of the destruction of his outpost at Front Royal. The next day, May 24, he was slow to move—according to the observation of one of his officers, "Because he was afraid to appear afraid." But finally he realized that if he didn't withdraw down the Valley immediately his entire force would be cut off and destroyed.

The Stonewall Brigade had brought up the rear during the march to Front Royal, but it was now in the advance, pointed toward Strasburg in order to trap Banks' main force. On the 24th Rebel units severed the Valley Pike five miles north of Strasburg, cutting off the rear elements of Banks' army. Huge amounts of stores fell into Jackson's hands. It soon became apparent that most of the Union troops had already gotten past on the pike toward Winchester so the Stonewall Brigade was put in pursuit. The 33rd and 27th Virginia Regiments were put in front of the brigade as it veered north.

In the spring of 1862, Jackson marched and countermarched his men for over 400 miles through the Shenendoah Valley, defeating three separate Union armies and tying down thousands of other Federal troops.

Belle Boyd was not a member of the Stonewall Brigade, but she became one of the most important spies in the Valley during the spring of 1862. She romped through the countryside on horseback prying intelligence from Federal soldiers and delivering it directly to Ashby's scouts. *(USAMHI)*

The night of the 24th was difficult for both sides as the retreating Federals found infantry and cavalry assailing their backs, while the Union rearguard staged several set-piece ambushes. After one of these nocturnal surprises, Confederate cavalry stampeded back through the 33rd Virginia, scattering the regiment and, according to its commander, Colonel John Neff, "creating for the moment a scene of most mortifying confusion." While the 33rd pulled itself together, Colonel A. J. Grigsby's 27th Virginia took the lead in the pursuit. But most of Banks' men had won the race to Winchester, where they tried to make a stand.

Jackson moved the Stonewall Brigade up the Valley Pike at dawn on the 25th, through a heavy fog. They were then sent in a sweeping movement over a ridge to the left side of the road to clear it of Union skirmishers. But there was a second ridge, more strongly held, and Jackson moved up artillery to take on the Union guns. A line of Federal sharpshooters behind a stone fence made havoc in the Confederate ranks, until Rebel guns switched from shells to solid shot to blast apart the wall. The Stonewall Brigade fought tooth-and-nail with the Federal center until Taylor's Louisianans circled briefly, then made a headlong attack against the Union right flank.

A few minutes earlier, Jackson had ridden to the positions of his old Brigade and had had to restrain the men from cheering him. Once Taylor's attack proved successful he said, "Very good; let's holler!" The Stonewall Brigade surged forward, and Banks' entire line became unhinged. His troops poured back into Winchester "in a disordered mass," and then out again, not stopping until they reached the Potomac River, which at its closest point was 25 miles away.

In Winchester itself the Rebels inherited another vast quantity of stores, reinforcing the nickname they'd already given their opponent, "Commissary Banks." The women and other citizens of Winchester were ecstatic when the Stonewall Brigade and other triumphant Confederate units appeared again in their town.

The only sour note for Jackson was that his cavalry had seemingly disintegrated during the fighting, mainly to safeguard captured horses. "Never have I seen an opportunity when it was in the power of cavalry to reap a richer harvest of victory," fumed Old Jack after he had witnessed Banks' men fleeing in headlong retreat. Nevertheless, the results of the victory were good enough. Banks had lost some 300 dead and wounded plus 2,300 captured. Jackson found another 750 Federals in hospitals and promptly paroled them. The Confederates had suffered 400 total casualties, including 37 from the Stonewall Brigade.

Although the battles of Front Royal and Winchester are considered to be distinct battles, at least one Stonewaller remembered it as one continuous fight. It did not end there, though, as the brigade pursued the Union troops all the way to Harper's Ferry. Jackson was interested

in keeping Banks cowed, and also in keeping Union authorities fearful of a Rebel incursion across the Potomac. Meantime, the bulk of his army enjoyed a well-earned rest, while the huge quantities of captured arms and supplies around Winchester were put aboard wagons for transit southward.

During operations in the Shenandoah Valley in 1862, the Stonewall Brigade captured hundreds of Union prisoners, who show their respect as they pass under the watchful eyes of General Jackson. *(Century Magazine)*

Brigadier General James Shields, a friend of Abraham Lincoln, attempted to trap the Stonewall Brigade during the 1862 Shenandoah Valley Campaign but could not close the vise on Jackson's "foot cavalry."

At this point, while the front on the Peninsula remained static, Jackson's sudden marches and surprise attacks had prompted alarm in the Northern press, while the same exploits had cast him as a hero in the papers of the South. The name "Stonewall" was fast becoming a household word.

The reaction of the War Department in Washington was to converge superior strength to destroy him once and for all. Fremont, having assembled his 15,000-man army, was ordered to invade the Valley from the west; General Shields with his 10,000 was ordered to re-enter the Valley from the east, to be followed by another 10,000-man division from McDowell's corps. These forces were intended to slice Jackson off while he was still around Winchester, cutting off his retreat to the south.

A race now began as Jackson, with his gigantic train of captured supplies, headed up the Valley Pike. The Stonewall Brigade, left northernmost at Harper's Ferry, was ordered to march hard to rejoin the army. Jackson stopped his force at Strasburg to wait for them to catch up, meanwhile fighting off advance cavalry probes from Fremont. Finally the bulk of the brigade joined him and the army continued south, though many stragglers were cut off and forced to the mountains to make their way back by roundabout means.

On the Pike, Turner Ashby's cavalry rearguard fought daily skirmishes with pursuing Federals. Other horsemen were dispatched east of Massanutten to destroy the bridges over the South Fork so Shields' men couldn't unite with Fremont's. On June 6, Ashby was shot dead in a rearguard fight, having gained as high a reputation in a brief time as any cavalryman of the war. But he had done his duty well. By then Jackson had escaped from the closing pincers and his army stood at the junction of rivers south of Massanutten—Fremont on one side and Shields on the other. Jackson could once again address his opponents in detail.

The Battles of Cross Keys and Port Republic, June 8–9, 1862

On June 8, Jackson's men fought on two sides, as Fremont approached from the west and Shields' advance units arrived on the east and north. That morning a sudden cavalry probe from Shields into the town of Port Republic made it across an unguarded bridge and almost captured Jackson himself.

Ewell's division, supported by other units, meantime stood against Fremont. Near the hamlet of Cross Keys, Ewell sent the Federals reeling with a loss of nearly 700 men as opposed to 288 Confederates. Fremont's men appeared shy of battle, and the famous Pathfinder himself was soon relieved of command. The Stonewall Brigade was kept closer to Port Republic, its Rockbridge Artillery firing away from across the river at Federal infantry and artillery that appeared near the town.

During the Valley Campaign, Brigadier General Turner Ashby's cavalry became the eyes of the Stonewall Brigade. Ashby had already become a legend when, on June 6, 1862, he lost his life in a rearguard holding action near Harrisonburg, Virginia. *(USAMHI)*

The Taylor House in Winchester, Virginia, became the customary stopping place for Union and Confederate armies during campaigns in the Shenandoah Valley. The hotel served as headquarters for General Jackson as well as Union generals such as Banks, Milroy, Sheridan, and others. *(Century Magazine)*

The next day, leaving Ewell with a reinforced brigade on the west side of the river to keep an eye on Fremont, Jackson switched his attention to Shields, whose advance brigades under Brigadier General Erastus Tyler had been pouring down from the northeast above Port Republic. Tyler's troops had seen the backs of Jackson's men at Kernstown the previous March, and were considered to be a tough outfit. In fact, the coming battle was to be the bloodiest one of the entire Valley Campaign.

At 5:00 in the morning on June 9, the Stonewall Brigade was passed across the river on an improvised bridge consisting of wagons weighted down by stones. Advancing north of the town for a mile and a half, they came upon the Federals, who were well posted. A thick infantry line supported by ten guns was waiting in a road that stretched from the river to a 90-foot height called the "Coaling," a plateau that had been cleared for the collection of charcoal. A battery of six guns was on the height, supported by two regiments of infantry.

When the Stonewall Brigade arrived at the position it became clear that the Union guns on the height dominated the entire plain. The Rockbridge Artillery was brought forward to suppress the enemy fire but started to get the worst of the duel. The 2nd and 4th Virginia Infantry, supported by Carpenter's battery, were peeled off to attack the height, but could not get close. The Coaling was fronted by a ravine and thick woods in front; Carpenter saw he couldn't get through the underbrush and returned his pieces to the plain. The 2nd Virginia was blasted on its approach to the height and fell back, its supporting 4th Virginia retreating in tandem.

Down on the plain, the 5th and 27th Regiments stood under a storm of bullets, shot and shell, losing dozens of men to the crossfire from in front and above. Colonel Grigsby of the 27th had his horse shot twice, and amidst his usual stream of profanity had to continue to fight on foot. As the morning wore on the Southern regiments began to run out of ammunition. The Federal infantry, sensing their opponents weakening, launched a countercharge and the brigade had to fall back. One piece of the Rockbridge Artillery was lost as a shell killed an officer and two horses just as the Yankees were a hundred paces away.

Meanwhile, Jackson had ordered Taylor's brigade from Ewell's division to flank the Union position on the Coaling. His rear regiment, the 7th Louisiana, was kept back and plugged between the 5th and 27th Virginia to help resist the Union onslaught on the plain.

Taylor found an unguarded path upward through the woods and found himself across from the Union battery, separated by the deep ravine. His men had barely gotten into line when he ordered a charge, and with a Cajun version of the Rebel yell the Louisianans ran down the ravine, up the other side, and overran the battery. Almost immediately, two Ohio regiments counterattacked and ran them out again. Taylor rallied his men and charged again, only to be thrown off the height a second time. The fight on the Coaling was hand-to-hand, Union cannoneers swinging their plungers while infantry fought with bayonets. Taylor launched a third and final charge, and this time the position was his. He captured five of the six pieces and was able to turn them on their former owners.

Back on the plain, the Stonewall Brigade had grudgingly pulled back but still held its formation, supported by other units that came into the battle. Once the Federals had lost their advantage on the Coaling, the entire Union line seemed to lose heart. The Confederates launched a charge that put Tyler's two brigades into a retreat that soon became a rout. The Southern troops pursued for five miles before giving up the chase.

At Port Republic the Stonewall Brigade suffered 199 casualties, 160 of them from the 5th and 27th Regiments which had stood on the plain. The 33rd Regiment somehow never made it to the battle; having been on picket duty the night before, it spent the day looking for the rest of the brigade. Jackson's entire force suffered 804 casualties and Tyler's Union force some 1,250, including 586 captured. Fremont pulled back, as did Shields, leaving Stonewall Jackson the master of the upper Valley.

The strategic implications of the Valley Campaign were more important than the sum of its tactical parts. In about 40 days, Jackson's

Probably no Union general suffered rougher handling from the Stonewall Brigade than Major General Nathaniel Banks, former governor of Massachusetts and one of President Lincoln's political generals. Jackson embarrassed Banks during the Valley Campaign and again at Cedar Mountain. *(USAMHI)*

men had marched 400 miles, won five significant battles against three separate Federal forces, captured thousands of prisoners and an untold wealth of supplies. Yet the real significance of the campaign was that a small army never exceeding 17,000 men had tied down 60,000 Federals, paralyzing even more for a potential defense of Washington. The result was that George McClellan's main force on the Peninsula would not receive its overland reinforcements. On the outskirts of Richmond, the Army of the Potomac would be on its own to face the combined forces of the Army of Northern Virginia.

The Seven Days Battles, June 25–July 1, 1862

Throughout the spring of 1862, the people of Richmond had nervously watched as a huge Federal army methodically advanced up the Virginia Peninsula, coming within sight of the city's spires. Consisting of over 100,000 men, hundreds of artillery pieces and siege guns, and supported by over 400 transport vessels and gunboats, it was led by the youthful general, George B. McClellan, dubbed the "Young Napoleon" by the Northern press.

The South's General Joseph E. Johnston had insisted on a gradual retreat down the Peninsula, since the immense power of the Union Navy

In early operations on the Peninsula, Jackson's brigade became blocked by the swamps of the Chickahominy and was compelled to make a tardy circuit before reinforcing the Confederate army defending Richmond. *(Century Magazine)*

After five hours holding off relentless Confederate attacks, Fitz John Porter's Union corps finally crumbled at Gaines' Mill, prompting McClellan to pull back his entire army from the environs of Richmond during the Seven Days' Battles. *(Library of Congress)*

could have outflanked any of his fixed lines, either from the York River to the north or the James River below. He had recommended drawing the Federals away from their naval lifeline and concentrating Confederate forces to fight a climactic battle at the gates of Richmond itself.

A key geographic factor for both armies was the Chickahominy River, which flowed from the northwest to bisect the Peninsula just east of Richmond. The most direct route to the capital was south of the Chickahominy, but in order to connect with the reinforcements he expected from McDowell, McClellan straddled the river, at first keeping most of his army on the north side.

On May 31, Johnston attacked the part of the Union army south of the Chickahominy. He was assisted by a huge thunderstorm the night before that washed out the bridges, leaving two Union corps isolated. The attack was well designed but failed in its execution, as the various Confederate columns couldn't coordinate their movements, some never making it to the battle at all. Still, with 6,000 Confederate casualties and 5,000 Federal, it was the largest battle yet fought in the East. Among the results was that McClellan was clearly shaken by a glimpse of the ferocity he would hence have to deal with; second, Joe Johnston was badly wounded during the battle and forced to cede command of the Confederates' main army to Robert E. Lee.

On June 23 a conference took place on the outskirts of Richmond, convened by Lee and attended by Generals James Longstreet, Ambrose Powell Hill, and Daniel Harvey Hill. A fifth general who arrived, disheveled and covered with dust, was Stonewall Jackson, who had ridden a relay of horses 50 miles since midnight to attend. Lee had made the decision to transfer Jackson's troops from the Valley to Richmond, thence to begin the destruction of McClellan's army.

The maneuver got underway with subterfuge, Chase Whiting's division from Lee's army boarding trains in Richmond with great fanfare in order to head west for the Shenendoah. Union spies witnessed the move (as they were meant to) and reported that Jackson in the Valley was being reinforced. Paranoia in Washington increased that while McClellan's main force was bogged down on the Peninsula, the capital itself was in increasing danger of attack.

Instead, Whiting's division, after reaching Gordonsville, simply returned down the rails to Richmond, followed by Jackson's entire force. The Stonewall Brigade had to march at first since railcars weren't available. But Jackson's men were used to this, and as John Casler of the 33rd Virginia said, "We could break down any cavalry brigade in a long march." After a grueling approach on foot, the Stonewall Brigade was able to board trains for the last 20 miles, disembarking just north of Richmond. Unfortunately they were still assembling on June 26, when the offensive was meant to begin.

The Seven Days' Battles actually began with a large probe by McClellan south of the Chickahominy in order to move his siege artillery closer to Richmond. On that June 25th he was fiercely opposed by Benjamin Huger's division, suffering over 500 casualties to just over 300 for the Confederates in a battle called Oak Grove. The primary

An after-battle shot of the ruins of Gaines' Mill, using the novel stereoscopic camera, which achieved a 3-D effect when viewed through special goggles. *(Library of Congress)*

During the spring of 1861 General Joseph E. Johnston arrived at Harper's Ferry to take command of the district from Jackson. The brigade organized by Jackson remained a part of Johnston's force until after First Bull Run, when Jackson returned to the Shenandoah Valley with a separate command. *(USAMHI)*

During the Seven Days' Battles the Confederates were constantly on the offensive, and though they suffered heavy casualties, were able to drive the larger Union army away from Richmond.

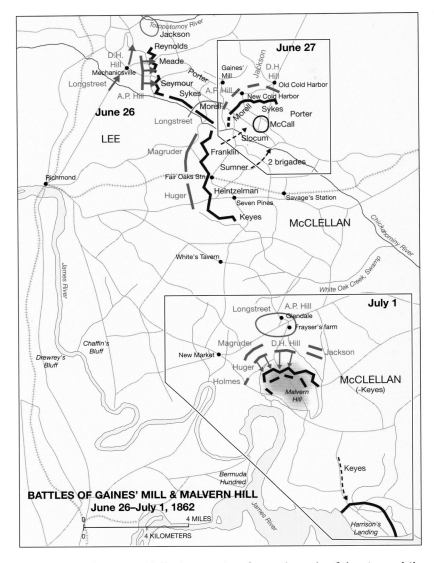

BATTLES OF GAINES' MILL & MALVERN HILL
June 26–July 1, 1862

result was to keep McClellan's attention focused south of the river while Lee's main strength shifted into position above.

Their target was Fitz John Porter's Corps of 25,000 men, which was the only Union corps still north of the Chickahominy. Porter had taken up a superb defensive position, however, and could be reinforced quickly by other Federal forces as well as supported by artillery from the rest of the army.

The morning of the 26th came and went, and Jackson still hadn't initiated the battle. At 3:00 in the afternoon A. P. Hill launched his own division in an attack on Porter's center near the hamlet of Mechanicsville. It was a bloodbath for the attacking Confederates, who suffered almost 1,500 casualties to the Union's 361. But Porter, now sensing his perilous surroundings, pulled back during the night to an even stronger position, just south of Cold Harbor near Gaines' Mill. His

The Army of the Potomac was never in greater danger than when forced to retreat across White Oak Swamp during the Seven Days, with Jackson and D. H. Hill in their rear and Longstreet and A. P. Hill on their flank. The terrain, however, was as difficult for pursuing Confederates as for the retreating Federals. *(Library of Congress)*

new position was on a commanding plateau on which he placed three tiers of infantry and artillery. At the foot of the height was a swampy, brush-covered stream that comprised a veritable moat.

On June 27, A. P. Hill again initiated the offensive, wave after wave of his infantry again being repulsed. Longstreet joined in on the right and then D. H. Hill on the left. Porter's corps on its height held fast, calmly mowing down Confederates by the hundred. McClellan sent over a division of reinforcements, and Union artillery fired at the attacking columns from across the Chickahominy.

Jackson had still not found Porter's vulnerable right and rear, as planned, though his units became gradually sucked into the battle. The 2nd and 5th Virginia were sent to the right to support a couple of Rebel batteries that were trying to dent Porter's line. They shortly rejoined the brigade for a set-piece attack from the north. The brigade had to make its way through dense woods and swampy ground, so that only the 2nd and 5th emerged in the clear in good time for the battle's climax.

Opposite Porter's center, John Bell Hood's Texas Brigade had arrived between 5:00 and 6:00, and subsequently launched one of the most important attacks of the war. Ordering his men not to fire a shot but to charge as fast as they could to get underneath the Union firepower,

Lieutenant General Richard Stoddard Ewell, who in 1862 supported Jackson during the Shenandoah campaign, lost his leg during the battle at Brawner's Farm. He returned to duty on May 23, 1863, after the death of Stonewall, and assumed command of Jackson's Second Corps. *(USAMHI)*

Hood and his Texans overran the plain, crossed the "moat" and then charged up the height. Finally allowed to fire, they blew a hole through Porter's line and poured in and among the Federal artillery. The brigades of Longstreet, D. H. Hill, Ewell, and Jackson, seeing the Union position start to crumble, renewed their assaults.

On the north flank, or Federal right, the Stonewall Brigade charged against a Federal battery that retreated before they could reach it. The colonel of the 2nd Virginia, James Allen, was killed in the assault, and 78 others fell dead or wounded, primarily from the 2nd and 5th Virginia. After dark it was a confused scene as Porter's corps retreated across the Chickahominy, destroying the bridges behind them, while Union stragglers and rearguards clashed with Confederate pickets. In one incident, members of the Stonewall Brigade went to a stream to fill their canteens, and upon being hailed for their unit, answered "33rd Virginia." A volley rang out from hidden Federals who then ran, leaving one dead and two wounded in the ambush.

Private Casler was on picket duty that night, and later wrote an interesting description of the main preoccupation of such after-battle duty: robbing the pockets or knapsacks of the dead. At Gaines' Mill there were plenty, as Confederate casualties totaled 8,750 and Union ones 6,837. Since nearly 3,000 Union troops were captured, however, the blood-loss was almost two to one against the Confederates.

June 28 was a lull in the Seven Days, as Robert E. Lee sought to mop up his gains, and McClellan began his "shift of base" south to the James River. All Federal stores north of the Chickahominy, and at depots on the York and Pamunkey rivers, were abandoned or destroyed. Lee, who had hoped to gain better fruit by severing the Union supply line on the York, was slightly slow to realize he had hit an empty bag, as McClellan had already determined to switch to the James. Nevertheless, a superb opportunity was still offered to destroy the Army of the Potomac during its cumbersome retreat.

As June 29 dawned, the armies presented a unique contrast. McClellan's force was still larger than Lee's, and had more and better artillery. It had, if anything, an excess of supplies, with an inviolable supply route via the Union Navy. Further, Federal officers had examined the terrain and roads, and knew far more about the Peninsula than the often-chaotic Confederates. The key to the campaign now lay in the minds of the commanders: McClellan already thought he was beaten and was dispatching depressed notes to Lincoln and Secretary of War Stanton. "If I save this Army now," he wired, "I tell you plainly that I owe no thanks to you or any other persons in Washington—you have done your best to sacrifice this Army." On the other side was Lee, who, albeit with an inferior force, had only a single-minded determination to make McClellan's greatest fears come true.

On the 29th, Jackson spent the day repairing the Grapevine Bridge over the Chickahominy so that he could pursue the Federal army, which was then strung out in a huge unwieldy column toward the James. Longstreet and A. P. Hill were dispatched back toward Richmond to cross on upper bridges, thence to hit the Union flank. The only action that day was launched by John Magruder, supported by Huger, at Savage's Station. Magruder pushed forward and inherited a Union hospital of 2,500 sick and wounded, but was not able to make a significant dent in the massive Federal column.

June 30 presented what Confederate artillery chief Edward Porter Alexander described as the very best opportunity the Confederates had to win the war in one blow. "Never, before or after," he wrote, "did the fates put such a prize within our reach." The bulk of the Army of the Potomac was still strung out across seven miles of a long, difficult swamp, burdened by its wagons, artillery, walking wounded and supplies. Lee had meanwhile positioned Jackson's Valley army, reinforced by D. H. Hill, on the Federal rear and left; Longstreet and A. P. Hill were on their right; Magruder, Huger, and a division under Holmes were nearest to cutting off the entire Union position at the James. The Confederates were in superb position to dissect and then destroy McClellan's force.

On that day, however, Jackson still failed to be energetic. On the approaches to White Oak Swamp he ran into Federal artillery and simply brought up some of his own guns to duel with them. The Stonewall Brigade had a day of leisure, even as they heard a roar of guns and musketry across the swamp. It was A. P. Hill and Longstreet, once again attacking the Federals on the right. It was the Battle of Frayser's Farm (or Glendale). They were able to destroy a division under John McCall (also capturing him), but were unable to stop the general

During the artillery engagement at White Oak Bridge during the Peninsula campaign, the Stonewall Brigade in the distance joins forces with Brigadier General Daniel H. Hill's division to assault the Federal artillery.
(Battles and Leaders)

withdrawal. Huger, Magruder and Holmes were ineffective, partly intimidated by Union gunboats now within range from the river. When an urgent call reached Jackson to advance, he replied, "I have more important duties to perform."

Jackson's behavior on the Peninsula has long been a subject of debate, many historians attributing it to a form of clinical exhaustion after the Valley Campaign. Porter Alexander disagreed, saying that Jackson had been inactive on the 29th only because it was a Sunday, and "had remembered the Sabbath day to keep it holy." Perhaps there is something to be said for the view that Jackson, having taken his own counsel for so long against great odds, simply didn't recognize the urgency of his movements now that he was part of the main army. For this Lee must share the blame for not issuing more crisp and urgent orders, or perhaps for not relying more on D. H. Hill if Jackson was in any way incapacitated.

After the Army of the Potomac's escape across White Oak Swamp, it took position on Malvern Hill, a broad, commanding height near the river. Fitz John Porter again controlled the defense, now with three corps, plus attached brigades and 250 guns, including the army's entire reserve artillery. The Confederates thought that they could concentrate their own artillery to contest the Yankee guns, but batteries only emerged singly, then were immediately obliterated by Union fire. Rebel infantry assaulted the position by brigades, each one decimated in turn.

The Stonewall Brigade spent most of that July 1 trying to take cover. Its commander, Charles Winder, said, "It was the most terrific fire I have ever seen. There was a continuous stream of shot, shell, and balls." When finally ordered to advance late in the day, the brigade had to wade through units that were giving up the fight and others that were just hunkering down. The brigade lost 124 men in the battle, mainly from artillery fire. The army as a whole lost some 5,500 dead and wounded.

During the Battle of Malvern Hill, Union batteries positioned near the crest sent volley after volley into the Stonewall Brigade attempting to charge the guns. *(Century Magazine)*

During the Peninsula campaign, one of Jackson's patrols moves down to the James River to reconnoiter the intentions of General McClellan's Union Army, which had withdrawn to Harrison's Landing. *(Century Magazine)*

After dark, the Army of the Potomac retreated again, this time to Harrison's Landing, an almost inviolable spot where it was supported by the guns of the Union fleet. The final result of the Seven Days' Battles was that the Confederates had suffered over 19,000 killed and wounded, as opposed to some 10,000 Federals. But the Federals had also lost over 6,000 prisoners as well as gigantic quantites of supplies and munitions, and not least their pride.

"We were lavish in blood in those days," said the Confederate D. H. Hill, when later reflecting on Confederate tactics. But though McClellan had been vanquished, it was clear that the Army of Northern Virginia needed to rely more on maneuver in the future than on direct assaults. Fortunately, the Stonewall of the Peninsula would never be seen again, and with Jackson as Lee's key lieutenant, the Army of Northern Virginia would now enter its days of glory.

Confederate Counter-Offensive

In July 1862, though still compelled to eye McClellan's army with caution, Lee soon decided that he could detach troops to the west in order to secure communications with the Valley. In fact, during the previous weeks a more serious threat had emerged on the overland route to Richmond. Major General John Pope had been transferred from the Mississippi theater to command a new Army of Virginia, consisting of McDowell's corps, the Union forces in the Valley and new formations, altogether some 50,000 men. He was already nearing the Rappahanock River, across which lay the Confederate communications network and easy approaches to Richmond.

Jackson's men were the first to move, dispatched west by rail to Gordonsville in July. There the Stonewall Brigade enjoyed some three weeks of camp life, nursing their Peninsula wounds while receiving food or clothing from their homes in the Valley.

On August 8, 1862, Jackson's foot cavalry, with Charles S. Winder commanding the Stonewall Brigade, take the dusty road from Gordonsville. After whipping General Banks at Cedar Mountain (Slaughter Mountain) on August 9, the brigade moved north, toward Manassas. *(Battles and Leaders)*

A sour note was provided by Brigadier General Charles Winder, who began applying draconian punishments to the men for infractions of discipline, especially desertion. In one case 30 men failed to answer a morning roll call and were "bucked and gagged" for an entire day. This meant being forced to sit with their hands tied around their knees with a stick thrust under the knees to pin the arms in place; a stick or bayonet was also tied to each man's mouth. After this particular humiliation, 15 of the men deserted for good. One of the punished men, John Casler, commented that the general was brave and skillful in battle, but "very severe, very tryannical, so much so that he was 'spotted' by some of the brigade; and we could hear it remarked by some men near every day that the next fight would be the last for Winder." Jackson, when he heard of the humiliations being inflicted on soldiers of his old brigade, ordered them stopped.

Battle of Cedar Mountain (or Slaughter Mountain or Cedar Run), August 9, 1862

By early August, John Pope, who had been continuing to receive reinforcements, had crossed the Rappahanock and was approaching the Rapidan. When his lead corps under Banks marched south from Culpeper, which lay about in the center between the two streams, Jackson decided to cross the Rapidan himself to give battle. He had his old division, temporarily commanded by Winder, Ewell's division and A. P. Hill's, which had arrived at the end of July.

On August 8 Jackson's men waded the Rapidan and marched north. The heat was oppressive. Many men collapsed from sunstroke and the column becoming strung out. The next morning they met Banks' corps astride the road near Cedar Mountain. The Stonewall Brigade was thrown left of the road while most of Ewell's division took position on the right where Jackson expected the Federals' main strength to be.

Order of Battle: Jackson's Division at Cedar Mountain

Left Wing, Army of N. Virginia	*MG Thomas J. Jackson*
Jackson's Division	BG Charles S. Winder (mw)
	BG William B. Taliaferro

Stonewall Brigade — *Col Charles A. Ronald*
2nd Virginia, 4th Virginia, 5th Virginia, 27th Virginia, 33rd Virginia

Second Brigade — *Col T. S. Garnett*
21st Virginia, 42nd Virginia, 48th Virginia, 1st Virginia (Irish) Battalion

Third Brigade — *Col A. G. Taliaferro*
47th Alabama, 48th Alabama, 10th Virginia, 23rd Virginia, 37th Virginia

Fourth Brigade — *BG Alexander R. Lawton*
13th Georgia, 26th Georgia, 31st Georgia, 38th Georgia, 60th Georgia, 61st Georgia

Artillery — *Maj R. Snowden Andrews (w)*
Alleghany (Virginia) Artillery, Hampden (Virginia) Artillery, Rockbridge (Virginia) Artillery

Cavalry: Robertson's Brigade — *BG Beverly H. Robertson*
6th Virginia Cavalry, 7th Virginia Cavalry, 12th Virginia Cavalry, 17th Virginia Cavalry Battalion, 2nd Virginia Cavalry *(detachment)*, 4th Virginia Cavalry *(detachment)*, Chew's Battery

(mw) mortally wounded (w) wounded

The battle began with an artillery contest and then the Federals surged across a wheatfield, breaking the Stonewall Brigade's right, held by the 33rd and 27th Virginia. It turned out that the Federal strength had been concentrated in woods opposite the Confederate left. The 2nd, 4th and 5th Virginia countercharged, however, veered right, and were able to catch the Union troops in flank. More Federals pressed forward and the battle hung in the balance until two of A. P. Hill's brigades came onto the field to support the Rebel left.

Some controversy ensued when Hill's men claimed they had passed a fleeing Stonewall Brigade on their advance, but it was only the small 27th Virginia, which had reformed after its first rout, and for some reason had broken again. The 27th was commanded by a captain that day, its intrepid commander, Colonel Grigsby, still recovering from an arm wound on the Peninsula. After Hill's arrival the Yankees finally broke and hastened back to Culpeper, leaving their dead and wounded on the field.

The battlefield at the foot of Cedar Mountain, where on August 9, 1862, Jackson defeated a forward corps of Pope's Army of Virginia. A bloody clash fought under an intense sun, its main effect was to switch Pope from being aggressive to overly cautious. *(Library of Congress)*

It had been a tough, bloody fight with Jackson losing 1,341 men (63 from the Stonewall Brigade) and Banks 2,381, 622 of whom were captured. Among the Confederate casualties was Charles Winder, who was mortally wounded by a shell while directing artillery at the battle's onset. "His death was not much lamented by the brigade," wrote Casler, "for it probably saved some of them the trouble of carrying out their threats to kill him." Nevertheless, he was deeply mourned by fellow officers who valued his worth. Jackson wrote in his report: "Richly endowed with those qualities of mind and person which fit an officer for command . . . he was rapidly rising to the front rank of his profession. His loss has been severely felt." Longstreet simply noted that, in Winder, Jackson had lost "his most promising brigadier."

William S. H. Baylor, former commander of the 5th Virginia, was named Winder's replacement, after members of the brigade petitioned Richmond for his appointment. It was the first time since Old Jack himself that the brigade was allowed to be led by one of its own.

The primary strategic effect of Cedar Mountain was that it knocked all the bombast out of John Pope. Henceforth he would be far more cautious, no longer stressing the offensive. This was prudent, because with McClellan evacuating the Peninsula. Lee and Longstreet were now free to join Jackson. It was a delicate chess game, because at first Pope had been intended to draw Confederate strength away from McClellan. Now McClellan had been temporarily wiped from the board and Lee was free to concentrate all his strength against Pope. The next move had to be made quickly, however, before the Army of the Potomac reappeared in force. Some of its units were already joining Pope, as was Burnside's corps from North Carolina, building Pope's army to 75,000 men. The Confederates had only a small window of opportunity.

Lee soon devised a plan to engineer Pope's downfall. While Longstreet remained in position to keep the Federals occupied, Jackson's corps would pull out and march west, then north to ford the upper Rappahannock. Then, screened by the Bull Run Mountains, he would cross that range to arrive in Pope's rear.

The Stonewall Brigade, whose division was now commanded by William Taliaferro (pronounced "Tolliver") was part of this column, which marched for two days and nights until it hit the Orange and Alexandria Railroad at Bristoe Station on August 26. The Confederates captured a number of railroad cars, as well as a large quantity of stores. Leaving Ewell's division as a rearguard, Jackson marched another four miles to Manassas Junction to find perhaps the richest prize of the war. Here was the main supply depot of Pope's entire army—acre after acre of warehouses and trains filled with every sort of edible, from hams to bread to Caribbean fruit. In addition, there were clothes, shoes, blankets, saddles, bridles, guns, ammunition and whiskey. Jackson tried to organize the distribution of articles, but his provost troops were just as hungry as the rest. He succeeded in draining most of the liquor before his men got their hands on it, but some enterprising troops found a substitute in the Union medical stores. Breaking into the packages, they found that each one contained small bottles of whiskey or brandy.

On the 27th, Pope realized that Jackson had turned his position and he abandoned the Rappahannock line, seeking to concentrate his forces against Jackson's isolated corps. The holiday at Manassas came to an end

Confederate foot soldiers traveled light. They carried a rifled musket, a cartridge box, forty rounds of ammunition, a bayonet, a haversack with a small amount of food, a canteen, and a blanket roll. *(Battles and Leaders)*

as the Confederates were forced to burn the huge quantites of stores they weren't able to carry off. Jackson withdrew his troops to a wooded area just north of the old Bull Run battlefield, after first sending A. P. Hill on a feint toward Centreville.

Back at the river, Lee and Longstreet began their march, following Jackson's route, as soon as Pope abandoned the Rappahannock. The Union general had, at best, two days to destroy Jackson before the wings of the Army of Northern Virginia were again reunited.

On August 27, 1862, after a week on the road and short rations, Jackson's troops dally at the Union depot at Manassas to pillage the vast stores of food stockpiled by General Pope's army. The haul included 8 pieces of artillery, 175 horses, 200 new tents, 50,000 pounds of bacon, 1,000 barrels of corned beef, 2,000 barrels of salt port, 2,000 barrels of flour, and more than 300 prisoners. *(Battles and Leaders)*

The Battle of Brawner's Farm (or Groveton), August 28, 1862

Throughout the 28th Pope sought to concentrate his forces, which now included Porter's corps, in the vicinity of Manassas. He outnumbered Jackson by three to one, yet strangely spent the day unsure of where the Confederates had gone. The various Union divisions marched and countermarched, somehow unable to find Jackson's 24,000 men, who were simply resting a few miles north of Manassas Junction.

Jackson, for his part, began to worry that Pope was purposely avoiding him. When Jeb Stuart reported Federal troops moving east toward Centreville (a result of Hill's feint), Jackson worried that Pope was seeking to unite with the Army of the Potomac, which had begun reassembling near Washington. The combined Union army of over 150,000 men would be too much for the Confederates to handle. Jackson had to bring on a battle immediately, even if Lee had not yet joined him.

Around 5:30 in the evening, a Federal division under Rufus King came marching down the Warrenton Turnpike, parallel to and just half

a mile from Jackson's position. The Federals' style of march indicated they had no idea that Stonewall Jackson himself was watching them, his entire corps in bivouac to their left. The Confederates ran out some artillery to fix the Federal division in place, but its leading brigade kept on marching. The second brigade in line, under Brigadier General John Gibbon, halted and its guns returned fire.

Gibbon commanded the only fully western brigade in the Union armies of the east. A fierce fighter and demanding officer, Gibbon had also given his brigade a unique identity by arranging special uniforms, most notably high-crowned black hats. Within the army the unit was referred to as the "black hat brigade," though after the battles of the next few weeks it would earn a more enduring sobriquet: "The Iron Brigade."

Assuming that the Rebel artillery only belonged to some transient cavalry, Gibbon dispatched his 2nd Wisconsin to chase them off. The 430-man regiment had gotten halfway up the slope when suddenly out of the woods emerged a Confederate line of battle, ranks closed, guns ready, with flags flying. It was the famous Stonewall Brigade. The irresistible force had met the immoveable object.

Many of the inexperienced Wisconsin troops fired immediately. The Stonewall Brigade held its fire until it had reached a rail fence about 80 yards distant, when it delivered a devastating volley along with a huge Rebel yell. "Within one minute," said a participant, "all was enveloped in smoke, and a sheet of flame seemed to go out from each side to the other along the whole length of the line."

The 800 men of the Stonewall Brigade blasted the 2nd Wisconsin for 20 minutes before Gibbon rushed in the 19th Indiana on their left.

When Jackson's command moved back to the vicinity of Bull Run in August 1862, the Stonewall Brigade secured a defensible position at Groveton that looked out from behind fences and ditches across an open field of fire. *(Century Magazine)*

Edwin G. Lee entered the Stonewall Brigade as a 2nd lieutenant during the formation of the 2nd Virginia at Harper's Ferry. Lee rose in the ranks to become Jackson's aide-de-camp at First Bull Run and colonel of the 2nd Virginia at Second Bull Run and Antietam. In early 1863 Lee retired because of ill health but returned to active duty in 1864 as a brigadier general. *(USAMHI)*

Now the odds were more than even for the Federals. The two sides stood in place exchanging fire, neither with any thought of retreat. Ewell threw in Lawton's Georgia brigade to the left of the Stonewallers, to be countered by the 7th Wisconsin. Trimble extended the Confederate line with his brigade, just as Gibbon put in his last regiment, the 6th Wisconsin, 500 strong. By now the Confederates had more men in the fight and a gap had opened between the 6th and 7th Wisconsin. Abner Doubleday, whose brigade had followed Gibbon's, offered two of his own regiments, the 56th Pennslvania and 76th New York to fill the gap.

Night was falling, the smoke was thick, and the two lines, within shouting distance of each other, continued to fire away. Some men were standing, others kneeling, and many more were lying down under a stream of musketry from over 5,000 rifles firing in both directions. Private Casler called it "a terrible fight," and said the brigade was "guided in our firing by the flash of the other's guns." It seemed, he said, "that everyone who would raise up was shot."

At one point John Pelham, artillerist of Stuart's cavalry, dashed in on the flank of the 19th Indiana and blasted the Hoosiers with canister from 100 yards. He was followed by A. G. Taliaferro's regiments coming in on the right of the Stonewall Brigade. It was curious that Jackson, so eager for battle, was unable to bring more of his force to bear to crush Gibbon's gallant troops. Part of the reason is that both Confederate division commanders, Dick Ewell and William Taliaferro (nephew of A. G. Taliaferro), were badly wounded. Ewell had to have his leg amputated. A. P. Hill, off on the left, was unable to participate in the battle.

It was one of the war's most notable clashes, two elite units slugging it out in parallel lines for hours, neither side willing to retreat an inch. Afterward a Confederate officer described the curious look of the battlefield. "The lines were well marked by the dark rows of bodies stretched on on the broom-sedge field," he said, "lying just where they

In a panoramic view from Henry House Hill on August 30, 1862, Union forces are seen charging across the Bull Run battlefield in an effort to oust Jackson's men, who are holding a railroad cut near Groveton. *(Century Magazine)*

had fallen, with their heels on a well-defined line." As opposed to most Civil War battles where bodies could be found in depth, after Brawner's Farm they were just found in parallel rows.

The Stonewall Brigade lost 340 of 800 men in the fight, including two regimental commanders, Colonels John Neff of the 33rd Virginia and Lawson Botts of the 2nd, both killed. The 2nd Wisconsin and 19th Indiana, most directly opposite the brigade, lost some 500 men between them. The Iron Brigade, in its first major action, lost some 800 of 1,800 men overall. Total casualties topped 1,000 for each side.

Strategically, the battle was without value except for one important factor. Now John Pope knew exactly where Jackson was, and the next day he would attempt to destroy him with his entire army.

Second Bull Run (or Second Manassas), August 29–30, 1862

Now that his seeming cloak of invisibility was off, Jackson arranged his troops to meet Pope's onslaught. He took advantage of an unfinished railroad cut, much like a trench, to position his divisions, Hill on the left, Ewell's division (now commanded by Lawton) in the center, and Taliaferro's (now commanded by Starke) on the right. Behind the cut was rising ground and woods, which provided Jackson's men both cover and good fields of fire against attacking Federals.

The Stonewall Brigade was held in reserve behind the Confederate right during the first day of the battle, and saw little action. The Union attacks were launched mainly at A. P. Hill's left, and after severe fighting were repulsed. Pope still hadn't been able to concentrate his full army, and later a huge controversy erupted because Fitz John Porter's corps had failed to follow orders to attack Jackson's right. The truth was that, unknown to Pope, Lee and Longstreet had arrived on the field about midday, extending—in fact more than doubling—Jackson's right.

On the morning of August 30, Pope still didn't realize the looming presence of Longstreet. He thought the new Confederate forces were behind Jackson, and in any case believed that Jackson himself was retreating. A flurry of movement behind the Rebel line, consisting of wagons of wounded headed to the rear, and troops pulling back from the railroad cut to the shelter of the woods, reinforced his view. For his part, Longstreet was hesitant to move with Porter hanging on his right flank, though he did send in a heavy probe under Hood toward the evening of the first day, which was then withdrawn.

It was not till 3:00 in the afternoon of the 30th that Pope renewed his attacks, still convinced that he had Jackson at his mercy. This time Porter, who had marched all night against his better judgment, led the assault against Jackson's right, followed by units launched on his left and center. The attack was announced with salvos of Union artillery, and then wave after wave of thick blue ranks crossed the field. A. P. Hill and

Brawner's Farm and Second Manassas: *Stonewall Brigade Statistics*		
Unit	*Men*	*Companies*
Aug 28	**1,576**	
Brigade Staff	4	
2nd Virginia	270	10
4th Virginia	401	10
5th Virginia	439	10
27th Virginia	183	10
33rd Virginia	279	10
Aug 29	**1,212**	
Brigade Staff	2	
2nd Virginia	212	10
4th Virginia	325	10
5th Virginia	339	10
27th Virginia	155	10
33rd Virginia	179	10
Aug 30	**1,210**	
Brigade Staff	2	
2nd Virginia	210	10
4th Virginia	325	10
5th Virginia	339	10
27th Virginia	155	10
33rd Virginia	179	10
Sept 2	**1,160**	
Brigade Staff	1	
2nd Virginia	196	10
4th Virginia	304	10
5th Virginia	334	10
27th Virginia	153	10
33rd Virginia	172	10

Lawton were barely able to hang on, the men, when running out of ammunition, throwing rocks at their attackers.

On Jackson's right, Federals found a seam between two brigades and broke through. The Stonewall Brigade was ordered to counterattack down the slope from the woods, but was blasted back by Union troops who now held the railroad cut. Baylor, the brigade's commander, grabbed the flag of the fallen color-bearer of the 33rd Virginia and yelled "Boys, follow me!" He was shot dead seconds later. A friend and fellow officer, Captain Hugh White of the 4th Virginia, who had attended a prayer service held by Baylor the night before, grabbed the flag himself, shouting for the brigade to follow him. White, too, was shot dead moments later, the colors draping his corpse.

Andrew Grigsby of the 27th Virginia was now the senior officer and rallied the brigade again. This time they overran the cut, forcing the Federals to flee in that sector. By late afternoon. however, Jackson's line was about to crack as Pope continued to throw in fresh brigades. Fortunately, Longstreet had arranged for a combined battery, 18 guns under Stephen D. Lee, to enfilade the Federal lines. Then, just after 4:00, he launched his own corps in a sweeping counteroffensive. The Federal left immediately collapsed in the face of one of the largest concentrated attacks of the war.

Darkness called a halt to the pursuit, and because of gallant stands by a few good Federal regiments on Henry House Hill and other landmarks of the old battlefield, the Federal retreat was more dismal than chaotic. Nevertheless, the Army of Northern Virginia had once more seen the backs of its enemies.

Pope's army trudged on the road back to Washington, where it gradually met oncoming units from the Peninsula. The only cheers heard were when news raced down the ranks that McClellan was again in control. The Army of Virginia was no more, as the primary Federal force in the east would once more become the Army of the Potomac.

Two days later, on September 1, the campaign closed when Jackson's corps caught up to the Federal rearguard under Generals Isaac Stevens and the famous Indian fighter, Phil Kearny. The Battle of Chantilly (or Ox Hill) provided a surreal scene, as a thunderstorm roared louder than artillery, and both sides, pelted with rain, fought in confusion. Both Federal generals were killed, and the final result was only to increase further the casualty lists of both sides. The Stonewall Brigade did not take part; that time it had already suffered large losses in the campaign.

Onward to Maryland

In early September, Robert E. Lee now found himself near the Potomac River with no Union force in his front. The decision was made to invade Maryland, a border state which many Confederates considered

A recreation of the scene as the Confederate army crossed the Potomac to the accompaniment of the tune "Maryland, My Maryland." *(Bethanna and Joe Gibson)*

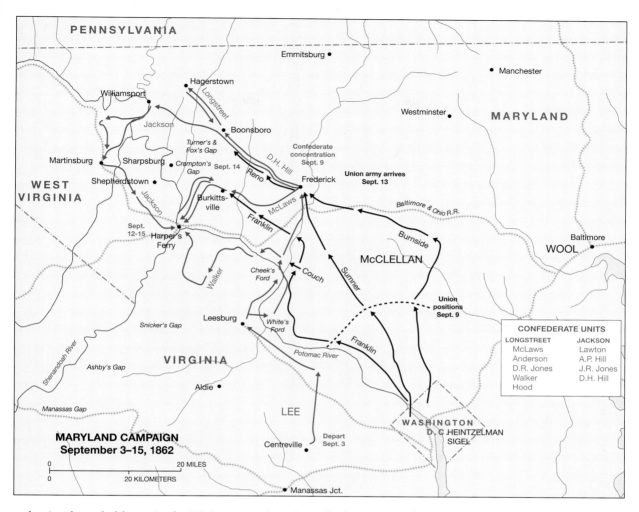

MARYLAND CAMPAIGN
September 3–15, 1862

as having been held captive by Union occupiers since the beginning of the war. On Maryland's untouched soil, Lee hoped for new recruits, new supplies, and a fresh opportunity to whip the Union army. In the west, the Confederate Army of Tennessee was on the march with similar hopes, on its way to invading the border state of Kentucky. In both theaters, it was now the high tide of the Confederacy.

As it developed, the Maryland campaign proved more to be the apex of Confederate straggling, as thousands of men deserted their colors, refusing to join the movement. Some were tired of fighting, some had had enough marching, and others simply had a philosophical objection to invading the North, since they had signed up solely to fight in the defense of the South. The 33rd Virginia's Casler, for one, dropped out after the recent battle at Manassas. "I found myself completely used up," he wrote. "I had slept but little for six days and nights, and was suffering with sore feet and hemorrhoids." He checked himself into a military hospital, but upon witnessing the horrors of the place, went to stay with an elderly farmer, one of the many who

In Maryland in September 1862, Lee scattered his forces and was then surprised when McClellan approached him with uncharacteristic speed, prompting the bloody Battle of Antietam. It was revealed later that McClellan had captured one of Lee's dispatches describing his movements—the famous "lost order."

ABOVE: During the Antietam campaign, the Stonewall Brigade participated in an attack on the Union garrison at Harper's Ferry that netted over 12,000 prisoners. Jackson positioned his artillery on Camp Hill, a plateau behind the town. *(Century Magazine)*

RIGHT: Another view of wartime Harper's Ferry. *(Library of Congress)*

At the start of the war Harper's Ferry was valuable as a crossing point for the Baltimore and Ohio Railroad, though both sides found the place strategically vulnerable. During the invasion of Pennsylvania in 1863, the Confederates simply bypassed it. *(Library of Congress)*

regularly brought produce to the hospitals in order to do their part for the cause.

For those who stayed in the ranks, the invasion of Maryland had its high points. One of Jackson's aides, Henry Kyd Douglas, wrote: "The passage of the river by the troops marching in fours, well closed up, the laughing, shouting, and singing, as a band in front played 'Maryland, My Maryland,' was a memorable experience."

Just like Bragg in Kentucky, however, Lee in Maryland was disappointed at his army's reception. It appeared that every young man willing to join the Confederate cause had already done so; meantime the populace was fearful, if not hostile, at seeing ragged Rebel columns bringing the war onto their soil.

Lee had expected that once he had outflanked the Union bastion at Harper's Ferry the Federals would abandon the place. Seeing they did not he split his army, Jackson's corps was assigned to take it, while he, with Longstreet and D. H. Hill, formed a front against the normally cautious McClellan, who was now following the Confederates from the environs of Washington.

For the men of the Stonewall Brigade it was another period of mysterious countermarching, since Jackson never revealed his intentions, not even to his senior subordinates. The brigade crossed back over the Potomac (this time to the band playing "Carry Me Back to Ol' Virginny") and took position on the heights below Harper's Ferry. Jackson's other units took position on heights north and west of the town.

The next day Jackson opened fire with his ring of artillery around Harper's Ferry, and the garrison almost immediately surrendered.

Falling into Jackson's hands were some 12,000 prisoners, 73 guns, 13,000 small arms, and innumerable stores. At this point Lee could have considered the campaign a success and ducked back behind the Potomac to Virginia. But he felt determined to make a stand at Sharpsburg, behind a stream called Antietam Creek, against an approaching Union army that outnumbered him two to one.

Leaving A. P. Hill's "Light" Division to take care of the Harper's Ferry captures, Jackson now countermarched to rejoin Lee. The Stonewall Brigade's 2nd Virginia was dropped off at Martinsburg to serve as provost troops. The rest of the brigade, now numbering no more than 250 men, arrived at Sharpsburg on the 16th. McClellan, true to form, had wasted another opportunity that day, as Lee had had only 19,000 troops at hand. Throughout that day and into the morrow the rest of Jackson's men, save A. P. Hill's, trudged in to take position on the Confederate left.

The next morning the battle began, thus far the bloodiest day in American history.

The Battle of Antietam (or Sharpsburg), September 17, 1862

When Joe Hooker's corps attacked in the early morning, the Stonewall Brigade was positioned in the West Woods, near a Dunker Church in a clearing that became the epicenter of the fighting. After blasting a Union flank, the brigade advanced into a clover field and was then beat down by superior numbers. One of its antagonists in this battle was the Iron Brigade, whose tall black hats were easily recognized on the field. Hooker was wounded and his corps repulsed, and then Mansfield's Union corps advanced. Hood's division arrived and counterattacked, killing Mansfield among others.

Early morning, September 17, 1862, the Stonewall Brigade rushes to defend and hold the turnpike fence supporting the left flank of General Lee's army at Antietam. (Battles and Leaders)

The Stonewall Brigade returned to the West Woods and found cover behind some rock ledges, firing away at thick waves of blue attackers. The fighting was so severe that Andrew Grigsby of the 27th Virginia (which according to one report only had 12 men on the field) was not only bounced to command of the Stonewall Brigade but Stonewall's old division, after J. R. Johnson was disabled and William Starke was killed.

Within a few hours the West Woods, East Woods, Dunker Church, and its nearby cornfield were covered with dead and wounded. The Federals on that end of the line called it quits, McClellan hanging onto his reserves while not realizing that one more push could have destroyed the thin Confederate line once and for all. The action switched to the center where D. H. Hill hung on tenaciously, his main position being a sunken road, afterward christened "Bloody Lane."

In the afternoon the battle shifted farther south to the Confederate right around Burnside's Bridge. The Federals finally forced the bridge, after also discovering there were passable fords both above and below it, and dislodged the Rebel right. The Federals, in massive force, were just on the verge of overrunning Sharpsburg and rolling up the entire Confederate position when A. P. Hill's men suddenly came onto the field, having marched all day from Harper's Ferry. Crashing into Burnside's flank, Hill sent the Union troops fleeing back to the creek.

Burnside's Bridge at Antietam, where the Federals finally pushed in the Rebel front, only to be counterattacked by A. P. Hill's division, which arrived just in time from Harper's Ferry. *(Library of Congress)*

Order of Battle: Jackson's Command at Antietam

Left Wing	*MG Thomas J. Jackson*
Jackson's Division	*BG John R. Jones (w)*
	BG William E. Starke (k)
	Col Andrew J. Grigsby
Winder's (Stonewall) Brigade	*Col Andrew J. Grigsby*
	Lt/Col R. D. Gardner (w)
	Maj Hazael J. Williams
2nd Virginia (det. at Martinburg)	*Cpt R. T. Colston*
4th Virginia	*Lt/Col Robert D. Gardner*
5th Virginia	*Maj Hazael J. Williams,*
	Cpt E. L. Curtis (w)
27th Virginia	*Cpt Frank C. Wilson*
33rd Virginia	*Cpt Jacob Golladay (w),*
	Lt David Walton
Starke's Brigade	*BG William E. Starke (k)*
	Col Jesse M. Williams (w)
	Col Leroy A. Stafford (w)
	Col Edmund Pendleton
1st Louisiana	*Lt/Col Michael Nolan (w),*
	Cpt W. E. Moore
2nd Louisiana	*Col Jesse M. Williams (w)*
9th Louisiana	*Col Leroy A. Stafford (w),*
	Lt/Col William R. Peck
10th Louisiana	*Cpt Henry D. Monier*
15th Louisiana	*Col Edmund Pendleton*
Coppens' (1st Louisiana Zouaves) Bn	*Col G. Coppens*

By evening some 23,000 casualties from both sides lay across the battlefield, 3,654 of them killed, not to mention the many hundreds who died later from their wounds. The Stonewall Brigade had lost 88 men, more than a third of its 250 who took part. The Army of Northern Virginia had fought perhaps its most skillful battle of the war, though it was now fought to a frazzle. Its remaining men were probably not larger than McClellan's uncommitted reserves, and 15,000 more Federals were on the way. Yet, on September 18, it was Lee who continued to hold the field, daring McClellan to attack again.

That night the Confederates finally marched back across the Potomac, their Maryland campaign at an end. In the North, the battle was interpreted as a rare victory for the Army of the Potomac, not least serving to provide an impetus for Lincoln to announce the Emancipation Proclamation, something he hadn't wished to do amidst the recent string of Union defeats.

Taliaferro's Brigade	*Col Ed. T. H. Warren*
	Col James W. Jackson (w)
	Col James L. Sheffield
47th Alabama	*Col James W. Jackson,*
	Maj James M. Campbell
48th Alabama	*Col James L. Sheffield*
10th Virginia	
23rd Virginia	
37th Virginia	*Lt/Col John F. Terry (w)*
Jones' Brigade	*Cpt J. E. Penn (w)*
	Cpt A. C. Page (w)
	Cpt Robert W. Withers
21st Virginia	*Cpt A. C. Page*
42nd Virginia	*Cpt Robert W. Withers,*
	Cpt D. W. Garrett
48th Virginia	*Cpt John H. Candler*
1st Virginia Battalion	*Lt C. A. Davidson*
Artillery	*Maj Lindsay M. Shumaker*
Alleghany (Virginia) Battery	*Cpt Joseph Carpenter*
Baltimore, (Maryland) Battery	*Cpt John B. Brockenbrough*
Danville, (Virginia) Battery	*Cpt George Wooding*
Hampden, (Virginia) Battery	*Cpt William H. Caskie*
Lee (Virginia) Battery	*Cpt Charles I. Raine*
Rockbridge (Virginia) Battery	*Cpt William T. Poague*

(k) killed (w) wounded

The best summation of the battle, however, was probably found in a statement made by Stonewall Jackson, who reflected: "There have been occasions when we have not been able to drive them; but they have never been able to drive us." This statement would hold true for the Army of Northern Virginia until the very last days of the war.

After Lee returned to Virginia his army quickly renewed its strength, in part because "the country was covered with stragglers from Richmond to the Potomac." According to John Casler (no stranger to straggling himself), "A few days after the battle in Maryland [Lee's] army was larger than it was during the fight." McClellan was so hesitant to pursue that Lincoln finally removed him from command, replacing him with Ambrose Burnside.

The Stonewall Brigade was quartered in the lower Shenendoah Valley during the fall, and a system of furloughs allowed many of the men to visit their nearby homes. Stragglers, convalescents and new

At Antietam the Union waves rolled up first against the Confederate left around the Dunker Church, then the center along the Sunken Road, and finally against the right, where a breakthrough around Burnside's Bridge was halted at the last moment.

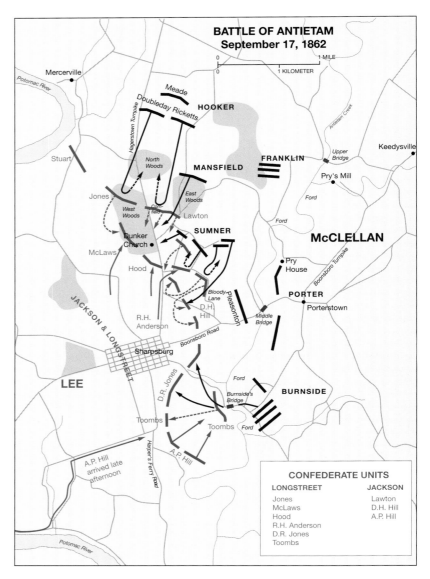

recruits soon swelled the brigade's ranks back to over 1,200 men. It took part in several raids on the Baltimore and Ohio Railroad, which passed near the Potomac, in which bridges were burned and tracks torn up. On October 16 the brigade had a sharp clash with a "nest of Yankees" at Kearneysville, losing three dead and 21 wounded, including the 4th Virginia's Colonel Charles Ronald.

The brigade's biggest disappointment that fall was Jackson naming one of his staff officers, Elisha F. Paxton, as its new commander. This was at the expense of A. J. Grigsby, former commander of the 27th Virginia, who had fought with the brigade since Bull Run and had commanded it at Antietam. To add insult to injury, the men of the 27th had chosen Grigsby as their colonel over the teetotal Paxton in the previous spring's officer elections.

The Dunker Lutheran Church at Sharpsburg, Maryland, shows the scars of Antietam and marks the road that the Stonewall Brigade used to reinforce the left flank of General Robert E. Lee's beleaguered army. *(Century Magazine)*

The most likely explanation for the decision was that Grigsby was a hot-tempered cusser—which Jackson strongly disapproved of—while the highly educated Paxton was, like the general, an extremely devout Presbyterian. Grigsby did not take the insult lying down and resigned his commission, though not before taking his complaint to Jefferson Davis himself, where he got into a furious shouting match with the President.

It is often noted that Jackson tolerated the incessant profanity of his chief quartermaster, but that may be because most of his curses were directed at mules. Richard Taylor remembered how at First Winchester, when under a hail of Federal bullets he had seen his men cringing and

With the Dunker Church in the background, an abandoned Confederate artillery limber keeps company with a collection of Confederate dead awaiting burial. *(Century Magazine)*

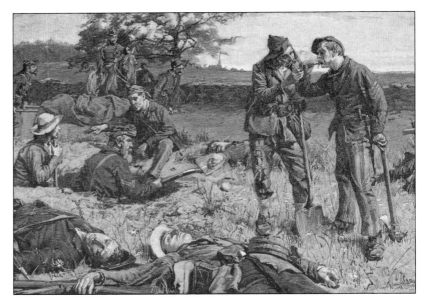

As night fell across the bloodied battlefield of Antietam, a general truce enabled soldiers, who a few hours earlier had been killing each other, to meet between the lines, light their pipes, and bury their respective dead. *(Battles and Leaders)*

yelled, "What the Hell are are you dodging for?" Suddenly he saw Jackson at his side, shaking his head sadly. "You are a wicked fellow," said Stonewall, who then rode away.

The Battle of Fredericksburg, December 13, 1862

On the first day of December the Stonewall Brigade marched to Fredericksburg on the Rappahannock, where the army was gathering to contest the Union's latest "On to Richmond" campaign. Now the Army of the Potomac, some 130,000 strong, was organized into three "Grand Divisions" of two corps each. The Army of Northern Virginia, numbering some 70,000, remained in two large corps, or wings, led by Longstreet and Jackson.

Brigadier General Harry T. Hays' brigade, supported by Brigadier General Paxton's Stonewall Brigade, waits beside the tracks at Hamilton's Crossing for the anticipated Federal advance during the Fredericksburg campaign. *(Battles and Leaders)*

LEFT: The town of Fredericksburg as seen from across the Rappahannock. *(Library of Congress)*

BELOW: Prior to the Battle of Fredericksburg Union engineers spent a day under sniper fire trying to erect pontoon bridges, until artillery on the heights behind them fired into the town, driving the Rebel sharpshooters to cover. *(Library of Congress)*

On the Rappahannock below Fredericksburg, Major General William B. Franklin's Left Grand Division placed pontoon bridges on the river to enable Federal forces to cross and assault Jackson's Second Corps assembled on the heights in the distance. *(Battles and Leaders)*

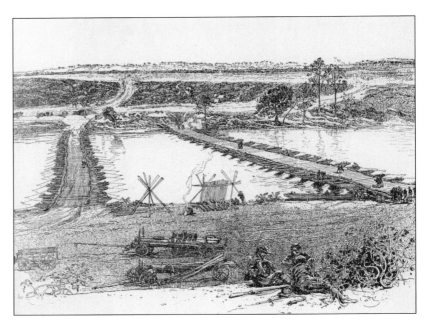

Lee had accurately divined Burnside's intentions, and by December 12 Longstreet's corps was behind Fredericksburg, mainly along Marye's Heights, with an infantry brigade behind a stone wall that ran along a road at the foot of the heights. A brigade of Mississippians under William Barksdale was in the town itself to contest the river crossing. Jackson's corps extended the line to the right, south of the town, facing woods and fields. The Stonewall Brigade, part of Taliaferro's division, was placed behind Maxcy Gregg's brigade of A. P. Hill's division, near a swampy woods that the Confederates considered impassable. To the brigade's nearest right was a division under Jubal Early.

On December 12 Burnside finally forced the river into the town, after blasting away Barksdale's sharpshooters, who had spent a day picking off his bridge builders. In front of Jackson the Federals were able to cross more easily since there were no defensible positions on the river, and the crossings were protected by Burnside's immense array of artillery to the north.

The next day dawned with a thick fog covering the landscape, though the waiting Confederates could easily hear Union officers giving orders, as well as the ominous rustle of approaching troops. Around 7:30 a Federal division under George Meade, flanked by Gibbon's and Doubleday's divisions, hit the Confederate front held by A. P. Hill. The Stonewall Brigade's Paxton saw Gregg's brigade giving way on its right (Gregg himself was killed) and Union troops breaking into the boggy woods, penetrating the Confederate center.

Paxton immediately counterattacked, the 2nd and 4th Virginia in the lead, and pushed out the Federals, who were now forced to take fire from three sides. Colonel Robert Gardner, recently promoted to command of the 4th Virginia, took a hideous wound to the face. In his report, Early stated that he had called for reinforcements from D. H. Hill to help plug the gap, but that the Stonewall Brigade had taken the initiative and gotten there first.

It had been a hard fight by both sides on the Confederate right, but by late morning Franklin's Grand Division had shot its bolt. The battle now shifted to the left where Federals emerged from the town of Fredericksburg across hundreds of yards of open space to assault Marye's Heights. This became one of the most gruesome killing grounds of the war as Rebels behind the stone wall and atop the ridge mowed down rank after rank of attackers. Six Union divisions launched 16 fruitless attacks until the field was covered with casualties. "It was not a battle, it was butchery," was a description that reached Lincoln's ears.

The Federals suffered 12,653 casualties at Fredericksburg as opposed to 5,377 Confederates, though this does not tell the full story of the slaughter. On Jackson's front it had been a fairly even fight; with 1,619 losses, A. P. Hill suffered more than three times as many casualties as any other Confederate division. It was in front of Marye's Heights that the battle was a Federal disaster, Longstreet suffering no more than 1,500 total casualties while the Federals lost at least 8,000. The Stonewall Brigade lost about 70 men, mainly to long-range artillery fire, among whom were only four killed.

In January Burnside continued to flail for an opening on the north side of the Rappahannock, but only succeeded in losing several thousand more men to sickness in what his troops dubbed the "Mud

After the Battle of Fredericksburg in December 1862 the Stonewall Brigade went into winter quarters, where the brigade was swept by a religious revival. (*Library of Congress*)

March." He was subsequently relieved of the command he had never wanted, and was replaced by "Fighting Joe" Hooker.

After the battle, the Stonewall Brigade went into winter quarters a short distance west of Fredericksburg. At the end of the year Paxton noted that during the course of 1862 the brigade had suffered 1,220 dead and wounded, or "more men than we could turn out for a fight today." The winter was primarily marked by a wave of religious revivalism that swept through the Confederate camps. Paxton himself became increasingly devout, constantly reading his New Testament. He arranged for the brigade to build its own chapel, releasing from normal duties the men who helped build it. Services were always well attended, often by Stonewall Jackson himself, though the general had a well known habit of sleeping in church.

1863

The Battle of Chancellorsville, April 30–May 6, 1863

The Union's next offensive campaign got underway in April, and was probably the most skillfully designed of them all. It also set the stage for Lee's—and Jackson's—greatest victory.

The Army of the Potomac had been rebuilt to full strength, about 130,000 well trained and superbly equipped men. Lee only had about 57,000 because Longstreet, with half his corps, was on a subsidiary operation and would not return in time for the battle.

Hooker's plan was to feint at Fredericksburg with John Sedgwick's corps of 30,000 men, hoping to pin Lee's attention. The bulk of his army would move up above the fork of the Rappahannock and Rapidan, ford both rivers to Lee's left, and then march east, uncovering other fords to allow still more divisions to cross. Lee would be caught in a massive vice.

In the last days of April Hooker's legions crossed the river into an area of tangled, wooded scrubland that locals called the Wilderness. After consolidating his army on April 30 he began to march east. In Fredericksburg, church bells pealed the alarm as Sedgwick's corps arrived opposite the town. Though outnumbered more than two to one, Lee had no choice but to split his army against the dual threats. He left Jubal Early with 10,000 men to hold the Federals at Fredericksburg while he marched to confront Hooker along the river.

On May 1 Lee's advance division met Hooker's van and delivered a brief but hard blow. Hooker, to the surprise of many, pulled back his forward units and consolidated his army at a spot called Chancellorsville and arranged his army for defense. Hooker still professed confidence, but by choosing the option of defensive tactics for the battle to come, he had done something far more dangerous to his army—ceded the initiative in the battle to the Confederates.

Federal forces advancing toward Chancellorsville by the U.S. Ford road on the night of April 30. *(Library of Congress)*

That night, Lee and Jackson held their last meeting, the two men sitting on cracker boxes near a crossroads in the woods. Jeb Stuart had reported that Hooker's right flank was hanging undefended, the Federals having no reason to expect an attack from that direction. It would take a long, roundabout march to reach it, with the danger that, if the Federals detected the movement, all would be lost. Jackson said

In early action during the Battle of Chancellorsville, Jackson's corps (in background) was caught off guard when it stopped at Hazel Grove to reform and unexpectedly came under attack from Major General Alfred Pleasonton's artillery. *(Battles and Leaders)*

With an all-day march on May 2, 1863, Jackson swung his corps around the right flank of Major General Joseph Hooker's Union army and stampeded Major General Oliver O. Howard's XI Corps down the plank road toward Chancellorsville. *(Battles and Leaders)*

he could make the march. Lee asked him how many men he needed and Jackson replied that he would take his whole corps. That would leave Lee with little over 20,000 men to oppose Hooker's main force. Jackson would be out of touch for the next 18 hours, making the most daring flank march of the war.

Jackson's men marched at four in the morning on May 2, first heading south, then west. With Stuart's cavalry screening the route they heard constant skirmishing to their right. At one point Union troops could see the column passing through a clearing, but they interpreted it as a Rebel retreat southward. Around 5:00 in the afternoon the Confederates arrived on Hooker's flank, which consisted of Oliver O. Howard's nearly half-German XI Corps, 13,000 strong. The Federals were idle, mainly occupied with cooking their supper. Jackson arranged his troops in three lines by division, that of Richard Rodes in the lead.

During the late afternoon of May 2, 1863, Major General Oliver O. Howard attempted to halt the Confederate attack on the Plank Road by throwing up breastworks, but Jackson's corps and the Stonewall Brigade would not be stopped. *(Battles and Leaders)*

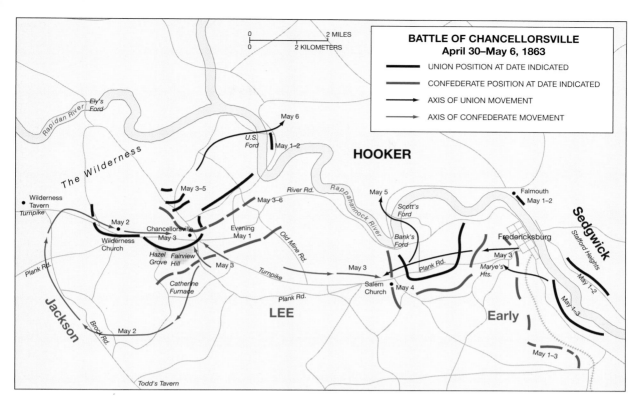

BATTLE OF CHANCELLORSVILLE
April 30–May 6, 1863

UNION POSITION AT DATE INDICATED
CONFEDERATE POSITION AT DATE INDICATED
AXIS OF UNION MOVEMENT
AXIS OF CONFEDERATE MOVEMENT

The first intimation the Federals had of the attack was a wave of squirrels, rabbits, birds and other wildlife scampering toward them out of the woods. Then they saw solid waves of graybacks screaming the Rebel yell, followed by a sheet of flame that tore apart their reverie. Within minutes Howard's corps had caved in and Jackson's men were overrunning their camp.

The Stonewall Brigade had been toward the rear of the column and was placed astride the Orange Plank Road, on the right flank of the assault. Most of the Federals had run before they arrived, so the brigade mainly had to wade through dead and wounded. Private Casler was highly tempted to loot some pockets but feared the flat of an officer's sword if he stopped to do so. He was, however, able to snatch a wounded Yankee officer's sword.

Jackson's intent had been not only to push in Hooker's flank but to insert his corps between the Union army and U.S. Ford on the river, thus cutting it off from retreat. As darkness fell he was still seeking to maneuver for this crucial advantage, and personally rode to the front to make a reconnaissance. Meeting a volley of musketry from hidden Federals, he and his staff turned back. A North Carolina regiment, hearing hoofbeats approaching, assumed it was an attack by Federal cavalry and opened fire at close range. Stonewall Jackson was hit three times—in the right hand, left wrist, and upper left arm, the latter wound severing an artery.

At Chancellorsville the Army of Northern Virginia was outnumbered two to one, yet General Lee split his force into three parts and won perhaps his most spectacular victory, after Stonewall Jackson caved in the Federal right.

In the dark and confusion at Chancellorsville, General Jackson was struck down accidentally by his own men, who mistook him and his staff for Federal cavalry. *(Library of Congress)*

The entire night was a scene of confusion on both sides. Casler reported that the Confederate assault columns had gotten so mixed up that the men started shouting, "hallooing for this regiment or that regiment." Yankee artillery batteries zeroed in on the noise with "the most terrible and destructive shelling that we were subject to during the war." Casler found a shallow hole and pressed his nose to the ground, shells and shrapnel whizzing just six inches over his head. When the Federals ceased firing, he said, "the men commenced calling their commands again, making as much noise as ever." The Federal batteries opened up anew, as bad as before, though fortunately didn't keep it up. If the Federal gunners had realized the execution they were doing, he said, "they would literally have torn us to pieces and nearly annihilated our corps that night."

This was the artillery fire that wounded A. P. Hill when he arrived to assist Jackson, and also knocked down the stretcher bearers who were trying to carry Stonewall to the rear. He was tumbled off his stretcher to the ground, aggravating his wounds.

That night the Stonewall Brigade braced itself for full confrontational battle on the morrow. There could be no more strategic maneuvers. Now that Jackson was disabled, as was Hill, Stuart had been put in command of the corps, and the Yankees would be waiting for a renewed assault.

Brigade commander Frank Paxton had a premonition of his death that night, and issued instructions about sending his personal effects to his wife. He was wearing a new brigadier general's uniform that he'd received two days earlier. Though Paxton had not been well received by the men at first, he had earned their respect and, in many cases, affection over the winter.

On the morning of May 3 the Stonewall Brigade formed into line of battle. Henry Kyd Douglas spoke to Paxton that morning and remembered, "Just before the brigade moved forward into the fight, he was sitting behind his line of troops, and, amidst the din of artillery and the noise of shell bursting around him, he was calmly reading his Bible and there preparing himself like a Christian soldier for the contest."

When the brigade advanced, the first obstacle they encountered was a line of South Carolina troops, already repulsed and refusing to renew the fight. With derisory comments the Stonewall Brigade passed over them, into the woods against a wall of Yankee fire. Paxton fell early in the attack, pierced by a bullet through the heart. His last gesture was to reach for the New Testament in his pocket, which also contained a picture of his wife. Hundreds of men, over half from the 4th and 5th Virginia, fell in the assault, and at first the brigade recoiled. But then, in cooperation with North Carolina troops, the Stonewallers attacked again until the Federals—dug-in behind breastworks—finally broke.

After the Battle of Chancellorsville Union wounded are evacuated across the Rappahannock under a flag of truce. *(Library of Congress)*

After nightfall on May 2 at Chancellorsville, Jackson attempted to make his own reconnaissance toward the Union lines. Mistaken for an enemy, Jackson suffered a mortal wound when a Confederate bullet shattered his left shoulder. The Stonewall Brigade lost a total of 493 officers and men at Chancellorsville. In no other battle did the brigade lose so heavily. *(Battles and Leaders)*

On the morning of May 5 the battered Army of Northern Virginia prepared to assault the remaining Union positions around Chancellorsville once again. It was an enormous relief, however, to find that, under protection of darkness on the previous night, Hooker, had retreated across the Rappahannock, leaving the Confederates masters of the field.

The battle had been one of the bloodiest of the war, with over 18,000 Union casualties and some 13,000 Confederate. The Stonewall Brigade had lost Paxton plus 493 men, nearly half its strength. The most grievous loss—for the brigade and the entire South—was Stonewall Jackson, who died of his wounds on May 10. Aside from the fact that he had been accidentally shot by his own men, it was a difficult loss because many soldiers had survived his type of wounds; it was actually pneumonia that dealt the final blow, aggravated by his loss of blood.

While still conscious in bed for several days, Jackson had asked for updates on the battle, and especially inquired about his old brigade. His aide Douglas conveyed the sad news about Paxton's death, but also described how the Stonewall Brigade had gallantly charged, even over the backs of other Confederates, and driven the Yankees from behind their breastworks.

"It was just like them, just like them," Jackson responded. "They are a noble set of men. The name Stonewall belongs to that brigade, not to me." A few days later Jackson died, after uttering a series of battlefield orders, calling for A. P. Hill in his delirium, and then finally saying calmly, "Let us pass over the river and rest under the shade of the trees."

The Confederates Invade the North

Longstreet rejoined the army about a week after Chancellorsville with his divisions under Hood and Pickett. Robert E. Lee found himself in a unique position, because for once after a major battle he was stronger afterward than before. Further, it was still the beginning of the campaigning season, and with the Army of the Potomac cowed yet again, the opportunity was presented to move the entire theater of operations into the North, finally relieving Virginia of having to sustain the burden of both armies.

First, though, with Jackson's death the Army of Northern Virginia needed to be reorganized. Previously consisting of two corps under Longstreet and Jackson, it was now divided into three corps. A. P. Hill was named commander of a new Third Corps; Longstreet retained command of the First Corps; and Richard Ewell replaced Jackson as head of the Second Corps. To the Stonewall Brigade, Ewell taking the place of the truly irreplaceable Jackson was well received. Though he had been out of the army for nearly a year after losing his leg at Brawner's Farm, Ewell was remembered as a skillful general who had worked expertly in tandem with Jackson during the brigade's early triumphs in 1862. Edward "Allegheny" Johnson, who assumed command of the division, was also a respected old friend from the Valley Campaign.

The men were disgruntled, however, by the assignment of James A. Walker as brigade commander after Paxton's death. Once again the Stonewall Brigade's own officers were passed over in favor of a brigadier from an outside unit. All five regimental commanders submitted their resignations in protest, though they were all rejected by Lee. Walker had in fact served with the brigade early in the war, but had then been assigned to A. P. Hill's command, where he was steadily promoted. A brave, muscular man who was not adverse to a drink, Walker eventually earned the men's respect. Still, since Old Jack himself, only once in the war had one of their own, William Baylor, been promoted to command of the brigade, and Baylor had been killed before even receiving his official confirmation.

On a positive note, while in bivouac at Camp Paxton after Chancellorsville, the brigade petitioned for and received an official recognition of its de facto name. On May 30, Richmond responded with a special order that read: "The Department cheerfully acquiesces

Brigadier General Edward "Allegheny" Johnson, though having a separate command, joined Jackson during the Valley campaign and caught a bullet in his foot. Following Jackson's death at Chancellorsville, Johnson took command of the division containing the Stonewall Brigade. *(USAMHI)*

in the wish expressed and directs that the brigade referred to be henceforth designated 'The Stonewall Brigade.'" The brigade thus became the only unit of its size during the war to have an officially recognized nickname.

The Second Battle of Winchester, June 13–15, 1863

In preparing for his next move north, Lee remembered the lessons of the Maryland campaign, which had been undertaken impetuously, resulting in as many stragglers as casualties. This time the army was given a full month to rest, recuperate and gather supplies. The Army of Northern Virginia was now at full strength with about 70,000 men and an even higher degree of confidence. During the early days of June it began to move north, Ewell's corps in the lead.

On June 10 the Stonewall Brigade passed from the area around Culpeper across the Blue Ridge to its beloved Shenendoah Valley. The citizens were ecstatic at the return of their sons, husbands and brothers, this time in the van of a triumphant gray-clad host that would liberate them anew from Yankee occupation. The men smartened their steps and unfurled their flags, as the brigade band played "Dixie" and "The Bonnie Blue Flag."

By the 13th Ewell's corps had arrived near Winchester, which had been under the draconian rule of Federal General Robert Milroy. Ignoring advice to retreat toward Harper's Ferry, Milroy had fortified the hills around the town and defiantly stood fast with 7,000 men. Ewell dispatched Early's division to the Valley Pike to approach from the south while Johnson's division, the Stonewall Brigade in advance, marched from the east. Union artillery and infantry outposts were pushed in, while Rodes' division came up and veered north.

The next day Early circled left to attack the town from the west. Coincidentally, his division included Taylor's old Louisiana brigade that had undertaken a similar maneuver at First Winchester the previous year. That day Rodes' division took Martinsburg with some 700 prisoners. Milroy now realized his danger, and shortly after midnight began to retreat north on the Valley Pike. Anticipating him, Ewell had ordered Johnson to dispatch two of his brigades north of the town to cut off the retreat.

That night a chaotic fight took place as Confederate infantry hammered the retreating column, throwing it into chaos. The Federal supply train stampeded, horses and wagons running over their own men. The center of the maelstrom was at Stephenson's Depot, four miles north of the town. The initial Confederate troops were outnumbered and had begun to run out of ammunition, when suddenly a tremendous Rebel yell was heard. It was the Stonewall Brigade coming on the scene, the 2nd and 5th Virginia in the lead.

Lieutenant General Jubal Early believed he could batter his way through any opposition and during the Battle of the Monocacy on July 9, 1864, used Colonel William Terry's Stonewall Brigade to spearhead the assault. Terry lost 59 of his 253 men, further reducing the strength of the shattered brigade. *(USAMHI)*

Order of Battle: Johnson's Division at 2nd Winchester

Second Corps, Army of N. Virginia	*LG Richard S. Ewell*
Johnson's Division	*MG Edward Johnson*
Stewart's Brigade	*BG George H. Steuart*
1st Maryland Infantry Battalion	*Lt/Col James R. Herbert*
1st North Carolina	*Lt/Col Hamilton A. Brown*
3rd North Carolina	*Maj William M. Parsley*
10th Virginia	*Col Edward H. T. Warren*
23rd Virginia	*Lt/Col Simeon T. Walton*
37th Virginia	*Maj Henry C. Wood*
Nicholl's Brigade	*Col Jessie M. Williams*
1st Louisiana	*Cpt Edward D. Willett*
2nd Louisiana	*Lt/Col Ross E. Burke*
10th Louisiana	*Maj Thomas N. Powell*
14th Louisiana	*Lt/Col David Zable*
15th Louisiana	*Maj Andrew Brady*
Stonewall Brigade	*BG James A. Walker*
2nd Virginia	*Col J. A. Q. Nadenbousch*
4th Virginia	*Maj William R. Terry*
5th Virginia	*Col John H. S. Funk*
27th Virginia	*Lt/Col David M. Shriver*
33rd Virginia	*Cpt Jacob B. Golladay*
Jones' Brigade	*BG John M. Jones*
21st Virginia	*Cpt William P. Mosley*
25th Virginia	*Col John C. Higginbotham*
42nd Virginia	*Lt/Col Robert W. Withers*
44th Virginia	*Lt/Col Robert M. Dungan*
50th Virginia	*Lt/Col Logan H. N. Solyer*
Artillery Battalion	*Maj Joseph W. Latimer*
1st Battery, Maryland Artillery	*Cpt William F. Dement*
Chesapeake (Maryland) Artillery	*Cpt William D. Brown*
Allegheny (Virginia) Artillery	*Cpt John C. Carpenter*
Lee (Virginia) Artillery	*Lt William H. Hardwicke*

Federal troops began to surrender by the hundred. Johnson's whole division rallied and soon swept the turnpike of organized resistance.

"Nothing could have been more timely than the arrival of the Stonewall Brigade," reported Johnson, and the fruits of the victory were immense. The brigade captured more men than were in its ranks and six regimental standards. With only 38 casualties in the brigade (3 killed), a member of the 27th Virginia called it "the cheapest victory [that] ever was achieved." Overall, the Federals lost some 450 dead and wounded

After the Chancellorsville campaign, the Stonewall Brigade—some with shoes and some without—begin the long dusty march on a road that leads through the Shenandoah Valley to Gettysburg. *(Century Magazine)*

and nearly 4,000 missing or captured. Ewell also captured 23 guns, 300 loaded wagons, hundreds of horses and an immense amount of supplies, all at a total cost of 269 casualties. The only disappointment was that the hated Milroy had escaped, fleeing on a white horse along with 300 cavalry.

Over the next few days, Ewell's corps crossed the Potomac, the Stonewall Brigade temporarily camping on the old Antietam battlefield. Longstreet's corps followed and then A. P. Hill's, after it was seen that Hooker's Army of the Potomac had abandoned its positions on the Rappahannock to conform to the movements of Lee. Jeb Stuart screened the march with his cavalry until June 25, when he received permission (or supposed he did) to take his command north of Washington and then make another of his celebrated circles around the enemy army.

Meantime, the Confederates spread across southern Pennsylvania, marching through Chambersburg, York and other towns, requisitioning supplies. Ewell made the northernmost incursion, reaching Carlisle. Outside Philadelphia and the state capital of Harrisburg, local militias built breastworks, and a bridge over the Susquehanna was destroyed.

Robert E. Lee had issued strict orders to the troops not to plunder, but his wily veterans were often difficult to deny. Private Casler wrote, "As soon as we would go into camp in the evening, some of the soldiers would strike out into the country, before they had time to put out a

When on September 3rd, 1862, General Lee ordered the invasion of Maryland, Jackson's men of the Stonewall Brigade were among the first to wade across the Potomac River at White's Ford. *(Battles and Leaders)*

guard, and would come back loaded with 'grub'." Naturally, any orchards along the line of march were picked clean, and woe came to any chicken that "crossed the soldiers' path."

On July 1 the Stonewall Brigade and its division received orders to rejoin the main army, which was assembling near a small town called Gettysburg. It was a slow, grueling march through heat and dust, and the brigade got tangled up in Longstreet's supply train. By afternoon,

On the forced march to Pennsylvania during the Gettysburg campaign, a Confederate soldier wounded at Winchester falls beside the road, leans his weapon on a clump of sod, and dies. *(Century Magazine)*

This map (opposite) well illustrates how the Army of Northern Virginia marched north and spread across Pennsylvania, closely pursued by the Army of the Potomac. When Jeb Stuart chose to circle the Union army rather than screen it with his cavalry, General Lee was forced into an unexpected battle at Gettysburg.

the boom of cannon could be heard in the distance. The Army of Northern Virginia had once again run up against the Army of the Potomac, and the greatest clash of the war had begun.

The Battle of Gettysburg, July 1–3, 1863

The battle began accidentally when two divisions of A. P. Hill's corps, probing eastward, ran into Federal cavalry outside the town of Gettysburg. The Federal I Corps under John Reynolds arrived, and then two divisions of Howard's XI Corps. The battle grew more intense, Reynolds being killed, until in the afternoon Ewell's divisions under Early and Rodes attacked from the north, crushing the XI Corps and forcing the remaining Federals to retreat through the town.

When Johnson's division arrived, the firing had died down and the men of the Stonewall Brigade were able to glimpse its aftermath. Several thousand Union prisoners were being rounded up, and the fields were covered with casualties from both sides. Amid the debris of battle, some Stonewallers may have noticed hundreds of the distinctive black hats of their old nemesis, the Iron Brigade, which had been nearly annihilated in the fight, losing more dead and wounded than any other brigade during the three-day battle.

The Union survivors had regrouped on a series of steep hills southeast of the town, where Howard had previously dropped off a division to build defensive works. Additional Union corps were arriving, having marched all day from the south. Around 6:00 Ewell received an order from Lee to take the central height, Cemetery Hill, "if practicable." With only one fresh division, Johnson's, an unknown force of Federals on the heights, and darkness about to fall, Ewell decided not to make the attempt.

That night it was decided to deploy Ewell's corps in a rough semi-circle around the heights south of Gettysburg—Cemetery Hill and its even more formidable neighbor, Culp's Hill—and place Hill's corps, reinforced by its third division under Anderson, to its right. The major attack on July 2 would be launched by Longstreet's corps against the Union left, which was posted on more accessible ground, though it terminated in two steep hills called the Round Tops. Ewell was ordered to attack in coordination with Longstreet's main drive, while Hill, who had suffered the most casualties on the first day of battle, demonstrated against the Federal center.

On the second day of Gettysburg the Confederates labored under several disadvantages. Jeb Stuart's cavalry had seemingly disappeared, and Lee had no idea how many Union formations were on the field or still on the march. Ewell, examining his new position in daylight, found that all his potential artillery emplacements were dominated by Federal gun positions on the heights. Longstreet's corps did not arrive on the

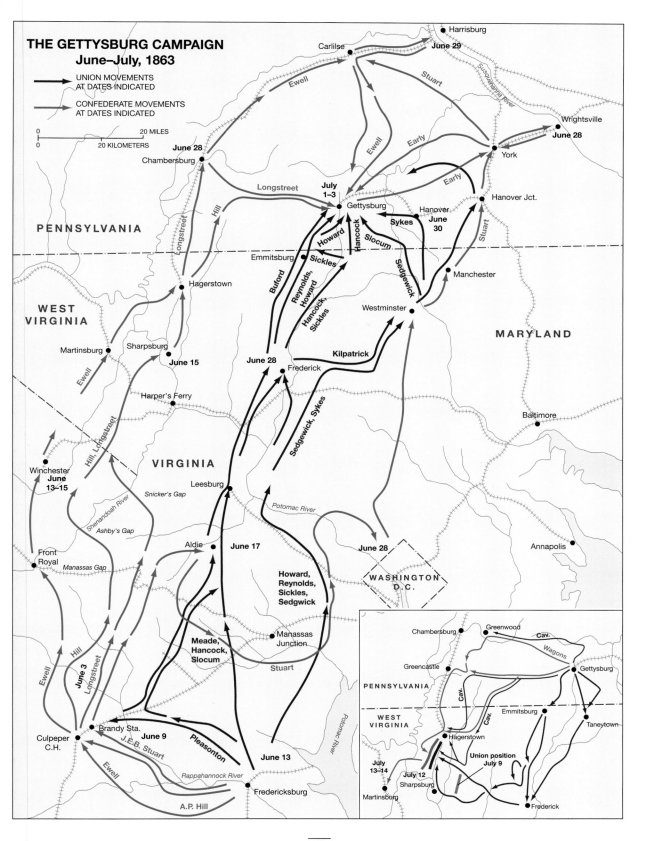

THE GETTYSBURG CAMPAIGN
June–July, 1863

→ UNION MOVEMENTS
AT DATES INDICATED

→ CONFEDERATE MOVEMENTS
AT DATES INDICATED

0   20 MILES
0   20 KILOMETERS

During the stifling hot march to Pennsylvania in June 1863, foot soldiers of the Stonewall Brigade pass a straggler from another unit who appears to be hiking along the Valley Pike in the wrong direction. *(Battles and Leaders)*

field at dawn, as desired, and even worse, Old Pete himself disagreed with Lee's plan. He had always opposed fighting a battle on the tactical offensive during this campaign, insisting instead that the army maneuver so that the Federals would have to be the attackers. His subordinate, Hood, was even more adamant against a frontal attack on July 2, his Texas scouts having reported that the Union flank behind the Round Tops was wide open.

Nevertheless, Lee stuck to his plan, and around 4:00 Longstreet attacked with his divisions under Hood and McLaws, supported by Anderson's division from Hill's. It was among the fiercest fighting of the war, across features such as Devil's Den, the Peach Orchard, the Wheatfield and Little Round Top. Longstreet pushed in the Union's III Corps and bloodied parts of four others, but at the end of the day he had gained only a few acres of ground. The Federals still held Little Round Top and Cemetery Ridge.

On the other side of the field, Ewell had found his artillery beaten down every time he set up a battery. The Stonewall Brigade was posted on the far left of the army, partly bent back to resist a flank movement by cavalry. At one point the 2nd Virginia was dispatched into a wood to flush out some sharpshooters. Some men of the brigade spent the day foraging in nearby farmhouses from which the occupants had fled for safety. One of the houses accidentally caught fire while troops were cooking rations on the second floor. "We regretted it very much," said Casler, and the men tried to save as many of the family's belongings as they could before the house burned down.

It was near dusk, around 7:00, when Ewell ordered Johnson's division to attack Culp's Hill. Since the position had been denuded of troops to face Longstreet, the Rebels were able to seize some abandoned entremenchments. The Stonewall Brigade, off on the far left, was not in time to participate. Even later, toward 9:00, Jubal Early launched an attack that overran Federal positions on Cemetery Hill; but because he failed to receive support, a Union counterattack ran him out again.

For all the calumny later heaped on Longstreet for his delay in attacking the Federal left, Ewell's attacks on the Federal right came off even later—in fact, after Longstreet's fight had finished and half the Union army was free to concentrate against him. That night George Meade, who had taken over the Army of the Potomac from Hooker just before the battle, held a conference of his corps commanders, at which it was decided to hold fast.

By dawn the next morning, the Union's XII Corps had returned to Culp's Hill and in a sudden rush reclaimed its entrenchments. Johnson's division was ordered to renew its attack, and now the Stonewall Brigade was foremost, advancing gradually up the steep hill, taking advantage of trees and large rocks to stop and return fire. Beyond a certain point, however, it was certain death to advance, as entire sheets of flame would engulf regiments who exposed themselves near the enemy's breastworks.

The brigade pulled back to replenish its ammunition, and Johnson ordered it farther to the right to charge alongside a brigade from Rodes' division. For the Stonewallers this was the most deadly part of the battle, as the closer they got to the crest the more murderous became the Federal fire. At one point a Connecticut regiment rushed down and captured over 60 men of the 4th Virginia who were hunkered down, unable either to charge further or retreat. Some men called out to the Union troops to hold their fire so they could come in as prisoners. James Walker finally ordered the brigade to withdraw from its perilous forward position, "as it was a useless sacrifice of life to keep them longer under so galling a fire."

The battle was over for the Stonewall Brigade, which had lost 318 men, about a quarter of its strength. Among the dead was a soldier of the 2nd Virginia, Wesley Culp, who had born in Gettysburg and whose relatives had owned the hill on which he died.

That afternoon the climax of the great battle opened with a gigantic artillery duel at the center of both lines. Casler described it as "one continuous roar. I could not distinguish one report from another." When Federal return fire began to slacken, some 12,500 Confederates, led by George Pickett's fresh division, marched in three majestic lines across a mile-long field toward Cemetery Ridge. Savaged first by artillery, then musketry, finally finding themselves in a gigantic crossfire, about 1,000 Rebels broke through the Federal center, but without support were swallowed up. The remainder, less than half, staggered back to their own line. In this attack died Richard Garnett,

During a lull in the fighting at Gettysburg, artillerymen supporting the Confederate brigades on Culp's Hill take a dinner break in nearby woods while waiting for a fresh supply of ammunition. *(Battles and Leaders)*

During the third day's battle at Gettysburg, the Stonewall Brigade and other Confederate units prepare to renew the attack on Culp's Hill, which protected the right flank of Major General George G. Meade's Army of the Potomac. *(Battles and Leaders)*

former commander of the Stonewall Brigade, who had been court-martialed by Jackson after Kernstown. Leading one of Pickett's brigades, he was last seen some 20 yards from the stone wall on Cemetery Ridge, but he must have been badly mangled as his body was never identified.

Total casualties for the three-day battle were staggering, with Union losses of 23,055, including 3,155 killed, 14,531 wounded and 5,369 captured or missing. The Confederates put their losses at 20,451, including 2,592 killed, 12,709 wounded and 5,150 missing; however, the Confederate returns may not have been complete.

After holding the field on July 4, Lee began to withdraw to Virginia. Though he was held up at the Potomac by heavy rains, the Federal army, save for some cavalry dashes, attempted no serious pursuit, and by the 14th the Army of Northern Virginia was back on its native soil.

Though jubilation erupted in the North at the Army of the Potomac's defensive victory, Lee felt that the campaign as a whole contained elements of success. He had brought back gigantic wagon trains of difficult-to-acquire supplies, including nails, hammers, forges, harnesses, shovels, shoes and saddles—all in addition to the food and forage that would otherwise have had to be taxed on Virginia. He had removed the Federal threat to Richmond for what turned out to be nearly a year, and had so damaged the Army of the Potomac that his own army was now free to reinforce other theaters.

Nevertheless, a temporary respite for Virginia was far from what Lee had really needed in the campaign. With the Confederacy elsewhere in decline, a resounding victory had been necessary in his theater to retrieve the new nation's fortune. This he had signally failed to achieve. As fought by the Confederates, the Battle of Gettysburg had been a study in discoordination, the various Rebel corps and divisions—even brigades within divisions—failing to act in concert.

The first explanation offered for the failure was instinctive throughout the South, and as such has been subject to the most counter-analysis across the decades since. But today's truth likely remains the same as the South's first instinct: If Stonewall Jackson had been alive to fight at Gettysburg, the Confederates would have found a way to win.

In September, Longstreet's corps was dispatched to the west, where it played a leading role in the Army of Tennessee's victory at Chickamauga. George Meade came under enormous pressure from Washington to attack Lee's diminished army, and in November crossed the Rapidan, seeking to dislodge Lee and open the way to Richmond.

During the Confederate retreat from Gettysburg, rain pelted the roads as ambulances—some marked "US"—bore the wounded away from the battlefield and toward the swollen Potomac. *(Battles and Leaders)*

The Army of Northern Virginia lay in wait near a stream called Mine Run, while Johnson's division with the Stonewall Brigade was ordered to the left to check a possible flanking movement. Suddenly Federals from Samuel French's corps burst from the woods and attacked George Steuart's brigade, which was leading the column. James Walker sent out a skirmish line of the 2nd Virginia to probe the Federals, who were now joined by part of Sedgwick's corps. The 2nd Virginia came under heavy fire and its commander, Lieutenant Colonel Colston, was shot from his horse. The rest of the brigade closed up, however, and Walker ordered a charge.

The opposing Federal line broke, but the Confederates found it prudent to stop behind a fence. Seizing a color, Walker jumped his horse over the fence and called on the brigade to follow. Yankee bullets whizzed around the general, but somehow he emerged unscathed. The two sides traded volleys until darkness fell, when the Stonewall Brigade moved back to replenish its ammunition. It had lost 154 men in the clash, including 20 killed.

After a few more thrusts and parries along the Rapidan, the Army of the Potomac gave up on trying to flank Lee and withdrew into winter quarters, as did the Confederates.

1864

During the winter months the Stonewall Brigade was swept by another religious revival, even as the hardship of campaign life seemed to increase. Many of the men's families in the Shenendoah were now out of reach, and the Confederacy as a whole struggled to provide proper rations.

General Lee himself was the recipient of many gifts from citizens, and for an entire month sent every pair of socks he received to the Stonewall Brigade. In a letter to his wife he wrote:

> I have sent to that brigade 263 prs. Still there are about 140 men in that brigade whose homes are within the enemy lines & who are without socks. I shall continue to furnish them until all are supplied. Tell the young women to work hard for the brave Stonewallers.

The most memorable action of the winter occurred on March 23, when a huge snowball fight took place. It was conducted in full military fashion, the Stonewall Brigade teaming up with the Louisiana Brigade against two brigades of Georgians and North Carolinians. Walker nearly got carried away by the excitement, and while yelling for a countercharge to an "enemy" cavalry thrust, got gleefully plastered from head to foot by the Georgians. Finally, the Stonewall Brigade's side won out, the deep South troops explaining that they were merely unfamiliar with snow.

But during the long lull since Gettysburg a more important event had occurred in the forces opposing the Army of Northern Virginia. Ulysses S. Grant had arrived from the west to be named commander-in-chief of all the Union armies. When the campaign season renewed, this victor of Fort Donelson, Shiloh, Vicksburg and Chattanooga would accompany the Army of the Potomac in its next onslaught against Lee.

The Overland Campaign
The Battle of the Wilderness, May 5–6, 1864

On May 3 the Army of the Potomac began passing the Rappahannock and Rapidan, roughly at the same points Hooker had crossed a year before. Except this time there were no carefully planned maneuvers; Grant's idea was attrition. He would seize Lee's army in a death grip and hold it fast until his larger force prevailed.

Lee knew from experience that the terrain of the Wilderness favored his smaller army. Artillery could hardly be used amid the thick, second-growth timber, and cavalry was relegated to the far flanks. Large infantry units were also difficult to maneuver and the dense cover favored the defense. He allowed Grant to cross the river, but his imperative was to keep him pinned in the Wilderness.

On May 3 the Federals crossed the river, and the next day unwisely paused to consolidate their units, while Ewell's corps on the left and A. P. Hill's on the right advanced to meet them. Longstreet's corps, which had returned from Tennessee over the winter, was posted some 30 miles away.

On May 5 the battle began just after noon as Governeur Warren's Union corps, supported by John Sedgwick's, ran into Ewell's corps along the Orange Turnpike. Farther east, Winfield Scott Hancock's large corps, reinforced by an additional division, encountered A. P. Hill.

On Ewell's front, the Stonewall Brigade veered right toward the nearest sound of firing. Suddenly its skirmishers were blasted by a hidden Federal line, hardly 30 yards away. Walker turned the brigade, but regiments had difficulty keeping in contact in the underbrush and gaps opened up. Just then a Federal regiment emerged and shattered the

The Battle of the Wilderness, fought May 5–6, 1864, comprised a maelstrom of close-quarters violence amidst smoke and dense woods. *(Library of Congress)*

5th Virginia, which fell back on the 27th, which was also disordered. The 4th Virginia was waiting behind, however, and when the cheering Federals ran forward they met a sheet of fire from concealed Confederates.

For the rest of the afternoon, the two sides exhanged fire as smoke enveloped the deep woods on what was otherwise a clear spring day. Colonel William Randolph, the seventh (and last) commander of the 2nd Virginia, was killed. Around 5:00 the brigade pulled back to replenish its ammunition, replaced in the line by Hays' Louisianans.

On the Confederate right, separated by a large gap from Ewell's right, A. P. Hill had likewise held back Hancock on either side of the Orange Plank Road. During the night, however, Hill, unlike Ewell, failed to order his men to construct works. He expected Longstreet to relieve him during the night, or at least by first thing in the morning. Meantime, under cover of darkness, Burnside's corps had come up and slipped into the gap between the two Confederate corps, his guns aimed at Hill.

Within a mere few hours on the morning of May 6, the fates of first the Confederacy and then the Union hung in the balance. At 4:00 in the morning, Hancock launched a huge set-piece attack on Hill. Burnside joined in, enfilading the Confederate line. The unprepared

In the tangled morass of trees and bushes, the Union and Confederate armies break into an opening beside a country road in the Wilderness and rush headlong into battle. *(Century Magazine)*

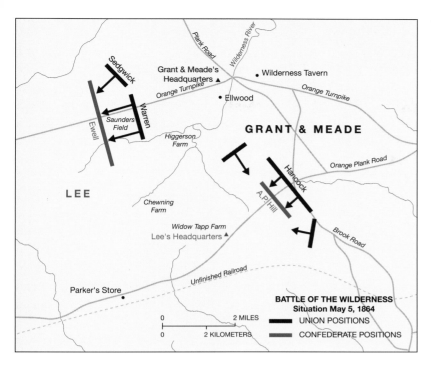

The first day of the Wilderness was fought in effect as two separate battles, until Longstreet arrived the next morning to restore the Confederate line.

Third Corps men couldn't stand and began streaming back en masse. They poured through the clearing where Lee had his headquarters, compelling the Confederate leader to plead for them to rally. Huge masses of cheering bluecoats began to appear from the woods.

Just then the sound of approaching troops was heard from behind. Trotting up the Orange Plank Road were fresh men, two parallel brigades with eight men abreast. As if on parade they split off right and left, waited for the exultant Federals to come in range, and then unleashed a solid wall of fire. Longstreet had arrived.

Hancock was stopped cold, his men now falling back as the rest of the Rebel First Corps came on the field. Hill's men rallied and were launched at Burnside in the center. After assessing the situation, Longstreet launched a flank attack and Hancock's corps began to roll up "like a scroll." At the very climax of the assault, however, lightning struck the Confederacy twice. Longstreet and his staff had ridden forward to reconnoiter when they were mistaken for Federal cavalry and blasted with a volley from their own men. It was within three miles, and almost a year to the day, since Stonewall Jackson had been struck down at a similar moment of triumph.

On the Confederate left, meanwhile, Ewell's corps had had little trouble holding off Warren and Sedgwick. Private Casler of the 33rd Virginia had helped make breastworks during the night, and of the fighting on the 6th he said that the enemy "was everywhere repulsed with great slaughter, as our men had gathered up all the guns from the dead and wounded, and had them loaded and ready for a charge."

Lieutenant Colonel Raleigh E. Colston commanded the 2nd Virginia during the fighting in the Wilderness in 1864. A few days later he was shot from his horse and mortally wounded at Spotsylvania.

The Battle of the Wilderness cost the Federals 17,666 casualties from over 100,000 engaged. Lee's 60,000 men lost about 8,000, the exact number difficult to determine because Confederate reports, never quite precise, became increasingly scarce as the war continued. Casualties in the Stonewall Brigade were unreported, as the unit was constantly on the move or in battle over the next few days, until a week later it was all but destroyed.

The Battle of Spotsylvania Court House, May 8–20, 1864

To the surprise of many on both sides, Grant refused to retreat after his repulse in the Wilderness. Instead he simply evacuated his wounded and put his army on roads to the east, toward a key crossroads at Spotsylvania Court House. If he could reach this position before Lee, Richmond would be at his mercy.

Lee sensed the movement, however, and won the race for the position. As the two armies confronted each other again, the Confederates built a long series of defensive works. Taking advantage of some high ground, their line bulged forward in the center, forming a position called the "Mule Shoe." It had been considered essential for the Confederates to incorporate the high ground, if only to deny it to Federal artillery. But for those manning the salient it meant they could be subect to enfilade fire, or unsupported if Grant chose to attack it head-on.

Ewell's corps was assigned to the Confederate center, and on May 9 the Stonewall Brigade took position on the left of the salient. The men immediately began reinforcing the breastworks, also constructing traverses for protection on the flanks. On the evening of May 10 an innovative Union Brigadier, Emory Upton, led a small but concentrated charge on the nose of the salient, breaking through. The Stonewall Brigade turned to the right and held fast against the intruders, Walker passing up and down the line on his horse encouraging the men. The Federals were forced out and the Confederates lined up to fire into their backs.

That night some of the Stonewallers crept into no-man's land to cut down pine trees, both for better fields of fire and to construct abatis on their works. The next day firing resumed all along the line as the Army of the Potomac probed for weaknesses. On the night of the 11th Lee sensed another large flanking movement and ordered the front-line artillery to be withdrawn and prepared for a quick move. The 22 guns guarding the Mule Shoe were pulled back and limbered up. The night was pitch black as a steady rain soaked the men and works. It was still dismal and raining toward dawn when the men detected the sounds of masses of troops in their front.

It was barely first light when shots rang out and Confederate pickets came racing in, yelling "They're coming!" Hancock's 20,000-man corps

Order of Battle: Johnson's Division, Spotsylvania C. H.

Army of Northern Virginia	***Gen Robert E. Lee***
Second Corps	***LG Richard S. Ewell***

Johnson's Division   *MG Edward Johnson (c)*

    Stonewall Brigade   *BG James A. Walker (w)*

       2nd Virginia, 4th Virginia, 5th Virginia, 27th Virginia, 33rd Virginia

    Jones' Brigade   *Col William Witcher (w)*

       21st Virginia, 25th Virginia, 42nd Virginia, 44th Virginia, 48th Virginia, 50th Virginia

    Steuart's Brigade   *BG George H. Steuart*

       1st North Carolina, 3rd North Carolina, 10th Virginia, 23rd Virginia, 37th Virginia

    Stafford's Brigade   *Col Zebulon York*

       1st Louisiana, 2nd Louisiana, 10th Louisiana, 14th Louisiana, 15th Louisiana

                           (c) captured   (w) wounded

After his repulse in the Wildnerness, General U. S. Grant continued his relentless attacks by shifting to his left, toward Spotsylvania Court House (illustrated), the North Anna, Cold Harbor, and finally Petersburg. *(Library of Congress)*

A fallen Confederate behind the breastworks of Spotsylvania's "Bloody Angle." It was here that the Stonewall Brigade was all but destroyed. *(Library of Congress)*

was attacking the salient. Within minutes, Johnson's division lined up along the works and the men leveled their rifles. When the oncoming wall of blue emerged from the gloom they fired—except that most of the pieces didn't go off. Their powder and caps had been soaked by the all-night rain. Union troops began to pour over the breastworks. The Stonewall Brigade had to fight on two sides, some against Federals rushing behind them and the rest against attackers still in their front.

The division's artillery pieces were rushed back into the salient, only in time to be overrun by Yankees. Much of the fighting on the breastworks was viciously hand-to-hand—bayonets, knives, musket butts and fists—as thousands of men swarmed together in a bloody melee. Walker, yelling like a demon, was shot from his horse, his elbow mangled. Allegheny Johnson was seen swinging his cane at a swarm of bluecoats. Bodies piled up in the trenches, the wounded under the dead, and then more layers of both dead and wounded. Blood and flesh mixed with rain and mud, creating an unspeakable mixture.

By 6:00 a.m. the Stonewall Brigade had disappeared, along with two thirds of the rest of Johnson's division. "All that escaped," said Casler, "had to run for it." (He himself had been in the rear fetching rations.) Some men, however, continued to hold out at the front of the works.

The carnage only grew worse after full daylight, as Confederate reinforcements led by John Gordon sealed off the base of the salient. Now Yankees were on one side of the breastworks and Rebels on the other, firing and stabbing at arm's length. The Federals had achieved a breakthrough but failed to exploit it; now they were sitting ducks as the

Confederates concentrated their fire, counterattacking and enfilading the men still clinging to the initial penetration.

After dark on the 12th, the Federal generals pulled back their men. Grant had failed to get significant subsidiary attacks going elsewhere. The Confederates finished fortifying their second line at the base of the salient, which would henceforth be known as the "Bloody Angle."

Grant continued hammering at Lee's Spotsylvania line for another week, when he finally called it quits and embarked on another flanking maneuver. He left behind some 18,000 more Union casualties while Lee had lost perhaps 10,000, including Allegheny Johnson, James Walker and 4,000 men from Johnson's division.

On the 14th the survivors of the Stonewall Brigade, fewer than 200, were consolidated with survivors of two other brigades—all Virginians—to form a single small brigade in Early's division. William Terry of the 4th Virginia, who had been wounded in the Bloody Angle, was named commander. The brigade was now less than a regiment-sized force, and painfully recognized as such, but its few remaining men would continue to serve, still referring to themselves as members of the Stonewall Brigade, until the very end of the war.

The Stonewall Brigade put up a courageous and desperate fight defending the salient at Spotsylvania's Bloody Angle, though afterward its survivors numbered less than a full-sized regiment. *(Battles and Leaders)*

Early's Counteroffensive, June 13–October 19, 1864

After Spotsylvania, Terry's brigade with the remaining Stonewallers was withdrawn to the defenses of Richmond. The campaign ended with Grant making nearly a perfect semi-circle to reach the rail center of Petersburg where he began a siege. Strategically, now that Grant had placed his army south of Richmond, Lee saw the opportunity to dispatch forces north once more toward the Valley and Washington, reawakening Federal fears for their capital, and perhaps to retrieve Confederate fortunes.

As Grant's bloody march toward Richmond continued, the Confederates continued to bar his way as above at the North Anna River. *(Library of Congress)*

Jubal A. Early was chosen to command the counterstroke, and in his remarkable, somewhat madcap, campaign in the summer and fall of 1864, he not only took back the Shenendoah Valley, launched another invasion of Maryland and raided Pennsylvania, but succeeded in bringing Abraham Lincoln himself under fire. The whole thing would have been more renowned had it not ended in disaster.

Having taken over the Second Corps from Ewell, Early marched his men from Petersburg on June 13, his first objective to take on Federal General David Hunter, who was threatening Rebel communications to the west at Lynchburg. The remnant of the Stonewall Brigade, now in a division under John Gordon, marched a hundred miles in four days, then boarded a rickety train to near its objective. Hunter fled at the

Confederates' approach, however, and Early turned north into the now-undefended Valley, the traditional invasion route for rampaging Rebel armies.

The Stonewallers were delighted to return to their home Valley, and as always throngs of cheering citizens turned out, though they were now thinner and more threadbare than before. On July 5 the corps passed

A stereoscopic view of the Cold Harbor battlefield. *(Library of Congress)*

Long after the armies had moved on, laborers were assigned to remove the thousands of Union casualties at Cold Harbor for reburial. *(Library of Congress)*

At Cold Harbor, Grant launched his troops in a fruitless attack against Confederate lines. It was here that fatalistic Union soldiers began pinning their names and addresses to their uniforms so that their bodies could be identified. *(Library of Congress)*

over the Potomac and veered east toward Frederick, Maryland. In retribution for depredations in the Shenendoah, Early levied a $200,000 tribute from Frederick (also $20,000 from Hagerstown), and then aimed his force toward Washington, DC. The capital was scarcely defended and the Federals called out clerks and invalids to man its fortifications. Grant was beseeched to send two corps of reinforcements.

On July 9, Early arrived at the Monocacy River where he encountered Lew Wallace with a scratch force of troops, reinforced the day before by a division of the VI Corps. The Federals had 6,000 well posted men to 10,000 first arrivals Early could throw into the fight. While most of the Confederates held the enemy in place, Gordon's division was dispatched across a ford to flank the Federal left. His leading brigades cracked the first Union line, then the second, but the third was the largest of all, extending beyond the Rebel flanks on either side.

At this point Gordon sent in Terry's brigade, including the Stonewallers. "This brigade advanced with great spirit and in excellent order, driving the enemy from his position," reported Gordon. For a brief moment it was just like the old days. Though Terry had to stand against terrific Federal flank fire, he held on to his breakthrough until other Confederate units sent Wallace's entire force into retreat. The diminished Stonewall Brigade lost 59 men in the fight, leaving their remnant at less than 200.

Early now marched through Silver Springs to descend on Washington from the north. On the 11th his advance skirmishers traded fire with Federals at Fort Stevens on the outskirts of the capital. His troops wanted to pitch in immediately, but only half of them were up, the rest strung out as stragglers along the hot July roads. Early could also see more Federal troops arriving by the hour, eventually 20,000 behind huge earthworks. Further, he knew that other forces were gathering behind him. He ordered a withdrawal, though Confederate sharpshooters hung around the next day to keep the Federals penned in. It was at this time that Lincoln, who had come out to observe the fighting, came under fire and a young officer named Oliver Wendell Holmes shouted to him, "Get down, you fool!"

On the 14th Early recrossed the Potomac, his men severely disappointed that they had just missed such a spectacular coup de main. Meantime, Confederate cavalry under John McCausland rode north to

The Battle of Cedar Creek on October 19, 1864, turned quickly from a Confederate victory in the morning to a resounding defeat during the afternoon, building up further the "butcher's bill" sustained by the decimated Stonewall Brigade. *(Century Magazine)*

Order of Battle: Cedar Creek

Army of the Valley	***LG Jubal Anderson Early***
Gordon's Division	*MG John Brown Gordon*
Evans' Brigade	*Col Edmund N. Atkinson*

13th Georgia, 26th Georgia, 31st Georgia, 38th Georgia, 60th Georgia, 61st Georgia, 12th Georgia Battalion

Hays'/Stafford's Brigade	*Col William R. Peck*

Remnants of 1st, 2nd, 5th, 6th, 7th, 8th, 9th, 10th, 14th, 15th Louisiana Regiments

Terry's Brigade	*BG William Richard Terry*

Remnants of 2nd, 4th, 5th, 10th, 21st, 23rd, 25th, 27th, 33rd, 37th, 42nd, 44th, 48th, 50th Virginia Regiments

---

Major General Philip H. Sheridan, U.S.A., became the nemesis of General Early's operations in the Shenandoah Valley. Over a period of several weeks during the autumn of 1864, Sheridan's army crippled the Confederates and reduced the Stonewall Brigade at Fisher's Hill and Cedar Creek to less than 200 effectives. *(USAMHI)*

Chambersburg, Pennsylvania, where they demanded either $500,000 currency or $100,000 in gold. The citizens said they couldn't come up with the sum so McCausland burned the town.

Now back in the Shenendoah, Early rested for a few days around Strasburg, then marched north on the Valley Pike. At Kernstown he encountered and routed a Federal force under George Crook. Just as in the Valley Campaign of 1862, the Pike became filled with fleeing Federals, abandoned wagons and burning mounds of supplies.

By early August the Federals had had enough, and on the 7th Major General Philip H. Sheridan was made commander of a new Middle Military Division, his forces to be called the Army of the Shenendoah. As Sheridan advanced up the Valley, Early pulled back from Winchester, drawing Sheridan after him until Lee reinforced the Second Corps with a division under Kershaw and more cavalry under Fitzhugh Lee. Now Sheridan retreated, until by August 21 he was back at Harper's Ferry on the Potomac. There had been only minor skirmishing up and down the Valley, but now the Confederates again had the Valley to themselves.

While Early vied with Sheridan, the situation at Petersburg had become more dire, and Lee ordered Kershaw's division and Richard Anderson's men back to the main army. On the other side, on September 15, Grant travelled to the lower Valley to confer with Sheridan, whose force now consisted of three corps of 40,000 men with over 10,000 cavalry. In the next few days Sheridan moved back up the Valley.

At the Third Battle of Winchester on September 19, Sheridan caught Early's four divisions of some 12,000 men strung out, and after a day of hard fighting the Confederates broke in disorder. Brigadier General Terry was badly wounded and the 2nd Virginia lost its flag. John Casler expressed disgust at the fight, writing:

Our line never gave back until both flanks were turned. General Early was to blame for the defeat . . . He ought not [to have] fought a battle with such odds, in that place, where the Valley was so wide and open. The corps never had any confidence in him afterwards . . . He would fight the enemy wherever he met them and under any circumstances, no matter if he had but one briade and the whole northern army came against him.

Federal losses amounted to 4,018 men, including about 3,700 dead and wounded. The Rebels lost 2,100 dead and wounded and 1,818 missing, the latter no doubt including a number of men who just scattered. Another setback occurred three days later when Sheridan caught Early at Fisher's Hill. Of Early's 1,235 losses, about a thousand were missing; the Federals lost 528 men.

For several weeks Sheridan felt himself master of the Shenendoah, and proceeded to devastate it according to the plan he had agreed upon with Grant, so that even a crow flying over would have to "carry its own rations."

During the fighting on Fisher's Hill on September 22, 1864, a few members of the Stonewall Brigade took sharpshooter positions in trees to pick off the enemy, but the effort failed to stall the Federal attack. *(Battles and Leaders)*

Somewhere along the line of retreat from Petersburg, the brigade gathers a little corn and stops momentarily to grind the kernels, mix the meal with a little water, and fry a few cakes before resuming their march. *(Century Magazine)*

On October 18 Sheridan's forces were encamped at Cedar Creek, about 20 miles south of Winchester. Sheridan himself had been called to Washington and had not yet returned. That night Early's army, led by Gordon's division, filed across the mountain on narrow wooded paths. At dawn on the 19th the Confederates surprised the Federal encampment, capturing a thousand prisoners and 18 guns, routing two of Sheridan's three infantry corps. Early tried to pursue but his men became disorganized, many of them stopping to loot the Federal camp. Sheridan returned and rallied his men, leading them in a counterattack to recapture their camp.

Of about 30,000 men in the battle, the Federals lost 5,665. Early may have had up to 10,000 men in the fight, of whom 2,910 were lost with over a thousand captured. After this latest defeat many other Rebels simply abandoned the ranks.

In December the Second Corps, less Early and a few regiments, was called back to Petersburg to participate in the dreadful siege. Cold, hungry and under constant fire, the remaining Stonewallers shared gloomy trenches with the rest of the Army of Northern Virginia, at first posted on the Confederate right. By March Terry had recovered from

After being pried out of Petersburg in April 1865, General Lee made a desperate march pursued by overwhelming Federal forces, until the race finally ended at Appomattox Court House.

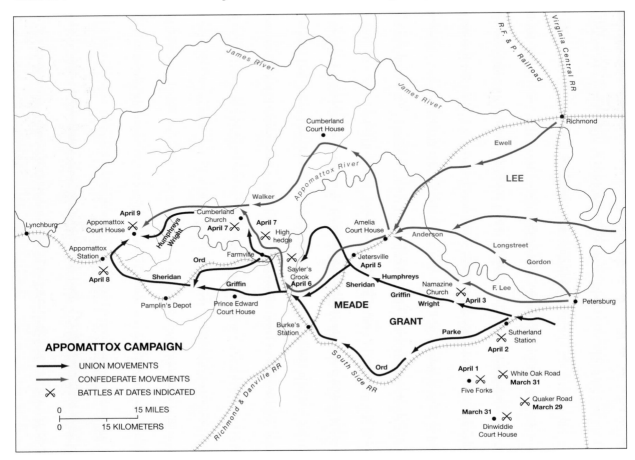

APPOMATTOX CAMPAIGN

→ UNION MOVEMENTS
→ CONFEDERATE MOVEMENTS
✕ BATTLES AT DATES INDICATED

0 — 15 MILES
0 — 15 KILOMETERS

his latest wound and the brigade was shifted toward the Confederate center near the site of the famous Crater.

On March 25 Lee made his last-gasp attempt to break the siege, aiming Gordon's troops at a Federal outpost called Fort Stedman. The pre-dawn attack briefly overran the fort, but then Union forces closed in. The 5th Virginia lost its flag and Terry was once again wounded, this time with a concussion. The Confederates had to retreat back to their trenches, pursued by sheets of Union musket and artillery fire. Now the end-game for the entire army was at hand.

On April 1, Federal infantry and cavalry destroyed Pickett's division at Five Forks, south of Petersburg. The town of Petersburg was no longer tenable, and neither was Richmond. Lee told Jefferson Davis that the capital had to be evacuated the next day.

On April 2, the Army of Northern Virginia began its last march, along the Appomattox River, Gordon with the remainder of the Stonewall Brigade serving as rearguard. The Army of the Potomac bounded from its trenches in pursuit. For a week the Confederates

The sounds of battle suddenly grew still around the village of Appomattox Court House on April 9, 1865. Federal and Confederate soldiers milled about the McLean House while General Lee signed the surrender terms offered by General Ulysses S. Grant. *(Library of Congress)*

Seated beside a table and with Colonel Charles Marshall (C.S.A.) standing behind him, General Lee listens as General Grant, seated center, explains the terms of the surrender. Brigadier General John A. Rawlins, Grant's chief of staff, stands behind the general's chair. Major General Philip H. Sheridan, whose cavalry blocked the remnants of Lee's army at Appomattox, listens from the far right. (*Battles and Leaders*)

marched and fought on almost no rations as the Federal army swarmed on their flanks. A. P. Hill, aggressive to the last, was killed in a skirmish. At Sayler's Creek on the 6th, Ewell and most of the Second Corps were cut off and captured, though Gordon's division was able to fight its way out.

Two days later, Gordon's men, now in the Confederate advance, encountered Federal cavalry barring their path and prepared to brush them away. But then the cavalry moved aside to reveal thick lines of Union infantry posted behind them. The Federals had blocked the Rebels' line of retreat.

On April 9, Lee met Grant at Appomattox Court House to surrender the Army of Northern Virginia. Grant's terms were surprisingly lenient. All he desired was for the Confederates to surrender their weapons and return to their homes on the vow that they would not again take up arms against the United States government "until properly exchanged." (This was a kind reference to the former parole system, which of course would disappear with war's end.) Lee asked if his mounted men could keep their horses and Grant agreed. The next two days were spent in writing paroles and issuing rations to the starving Confederates. Although 27,805 were present, Gordon later estimated that by the last day only about 8,000 under he and Longstreet had still been able to fight.

On April 12 the final ceremony took place as the Army of Northern Virginia stacked its flags and arms. Gordon's men, with the few survivors of the Stonewall Brigade in advance, were given the honor of leading the final march. Grant ordered no cheering from the onlooking

While soldiers wait for the outcome of the meeting in the McLean House, Federal troops come forward to share their rations with the half-starved Confederates. During a muster taken on April 12, only 210 men remained of the Stonewall Brigade's original five regiments. *(Battles and Leaders)*

Union soldiers, and in fact they stood in solid ranks and solemnly presented arms in salute.

The war between Americans had ended, both victors and vanquished arriving at a sense of mutual respect that would eventually result in an even greater Union. But the cost had been fearsomely high. Out of the approximately 6,000 men who served in the Stonewall Brigade during the course of the Civil War, only 210 remained at the surrender.

The bittersweet moment arrived when a Confederate trooper riding bareback galloped past a column of his bedraggled comrades, shouting, "Lee has surrendered to Grant!" *(Battles and Leaders)*

EQUIPMENT & WEAPONS

Samuel S. Sours of the 2nd Virginia was a typical private in the Stonewall Brigade. He wore whatever clothes he could find or borrow, often went without shoes, but took very good care of his musket. *(USAMHI)*

The sudden need to raise an army following Virginia's secession in April 1861 meant that there was little time to equip the men who volunteered in their thousands. As Jefferson Davis stated, "In equipping the armies first sent into the field, the supply of accessories was embarrassingly scant." Units were put together at incredible speed, and very few had the luxury of basic items such as uniforms or modern rifles, not to mention accoutrements.

The Stonewall Brigade began in just such a way, with the members of various pre-war militias being amalgamated with farm boys, merchants, craftsmen and college students. The militiamen at least tended to have uniforms, though these varied widely between communities. A number of units had been issued either gray single-breasted frock coats and gray trousers, per the 1858–59 Virginia militia uniform regulations, or blue frock coats in line with the 1860 regulations; but others had simply made up their own styles prior to the war.

Local newspapers of the day carried instructions detailing what the recruits should take with them, and also new regulations for dress. Most of the clothing was sewn by local women, who worked night and day—

A Soldier's Needs

From a newspaper article published in Staunton, June 7, 1861:

The following is a list of articles necessary to a soldier's comfort. Bring all of them you can, or the best substitute you can obtain: Two flannel over-shirts, 2 woollen under shirts, 2 pair white cotton drawers, 2 pair woollen socks, 2 pair cotton socks, 2 colored handkerchiefs, 2 pair stout shoes, 3 towels, one blanket (hole in the middle), 1 blanket for cover, 1 broad brim hat, 1 pound castile soap, 2 pounds bar soap, one belt knife, some stout linen thread, large needles, thimble and a bit of bees wax; some buttons, and some paper of pins, all in a small buckskin or stout cloth bag, 1 overcoat, 1 painted canvas cloth, 7 feet 4 inches long and 5 feet wide.

---

often in communal groups—to ensure that the men would not go without uniforms. Since supplies of cloth were limited, the seamstresses used more or less whatever came to hand. Consequently, the clothes they produced varied considerably.

As the various units began assembling, the different approaches to providing uniforms and equipment became evident. The Augusta Riflemen, for instance, were well kitted-out with uniforms bought using public funds at a cost of between $300 and $500. According to the Staunton newspaper, *The Vindicator*, of April 26, 1861, these were made in their hometown wool factory by Messrs. Crawford & Co. The Mountain Guards, on the other hand, were said to have left home with only a fatigue uniform composed of a red flannel shirt and gray pants. The Augusta Greys were in worse shape, having "Uniforms in bad condition of gray woollen goods."

Once the war was under way, uniforms became more standardized, with hundreds of thousands of items being manufactured in the factories of Virginia, North Carolina, Georgia and elsewhere, supervised by the Richmond Clothing Bureau and distributed by the Confederate Quartermaster Corps. Still, clothing continued to be sewn by local women, with large quantities coming, for example, from Staunton in the Shenendoah Valley because that town remained largely free of Federal occupation.

The basic kit to be issued a fully-equipped soldier would consist of a cap, jacket, shirt, pants, belt, shoes, cap box, cartridge box, bayonet and scabbard, canteen, haversack or knapsack, blanket roll and, of course, a gun. These items were naturally supplemented by any equipment the troops could seize from captured Union soldiers or depots, or scavenge from the battlefields. As the war went on, Federal-issued equipment became as prevalent in the ranks as that issued by the Confederacy.

Uniforms

Jackets Most infantrymen had a shell jacket made of wool, denim cloth, kersey (a blue-gray woollen fabric imported from England) or cassimere (a plain or twilled woollen cloth). After late 1862 wool was in short supply, and denim cloth and cassimere predominated. The cloth was usually colored with a natural dye made from the husk of the white walnut. This yellowish color, called butternut, became the true color of Confederate infantrymen, if not their officers who could still afford gray. Buttons were typically of brass.

Several patterns of jackets were made. Richmond Depot Type I jackets were most likely made from 1861 through the spring of 1862. Richmond Depot Type II and Type III jackets were more or less the same except that the later version (made from about mid-1864 onward)

First Manassas battlefield reenactment. Posed for his portrait is a sergeant of the Liberty Hall Volunteers. He is wearing the militia uniform of his company. For this first major battle of the Civil War, many Confederate units were wearing the uniform of their home militia, and militia uniforms varied widely from unit to unit. The Liberty Hall Volunteers wore blue kepi caps with the initials "LHV" in brass letters. Also this company wore battle shirts (not coats or tunics), in a blue-gray wool. *(Bethanna and Joe Gibson)*

An officer speaks to men of his unit at Pitzer's Woods during a reenactment on the Gettysburg battlefield. *(Bethanna and Joe Gibson)*

did not have shoulder straps or belt loops. They were made from six pieces of cloth, with two-piece sleeves and nine buttons.

From mid-1863 onward, another type became available, known as the Peter Tait jacket—the name coming from that of the clothier who supplied them. Although this was known as the English pattern, it was actually made in Limerick, Ireland. It was constructed from five main pieces, with two-piece sleeves and eight buttons. It was usually lined with linen. Documentary evidence suggests that the Stonewall Brigade was issued with uniforms of British origin at least twice during the years 1864–65.

Shirts Three different types of shirts were issued—made of wool or flannel (military or civilian pattern), overshirts, and cotton shirts.

Pants The pants that were issued to the troops by the Richmond Clothing Bureau were made of brown wool, others were to civilian patterns, usually butternut.

Belts Belts were made of black leather or canvas treated with tar, and were fitted with a variety of different buckles, most of which were made of brass. These were important pieces of equipment since other items such as cap boxes needed to be hung from them. The large front buckles were often inscribed with the initials "CSA," or the initials of individual states from which they were issued.

Shoes Although black or brown leather shoes were issued to the Confederate troops, many ended up with bare feet as a consequence of their long-distance marches along bad roads. Many in this position scavenged replacements from the battlefield or captured supply trains. It was not unknown for paroled Union prisoners to be relieved of their footwear. Standard issue patterns included the Jefferson Bootee and the Low Quarter British Import Shoe.

Hats and Caps   The most common style of cap was the kepi (which Jackson himself wore), though once government supplies faltered the men resorted to headgear of their own, most often the slouch hat; sometimes these would be fitted with ribbon trimmings.

Cartridge Boxes and Cap Boxes   Cartridges were kept in boxes made of black leather or canvas treated with tar. The three predominant styles were known as the 1839 Pattern, the 1857 Pattern (both of which the Richmond Arsenal copied) and the Enfield Pattern. A smaller version of the cartridge box was used to carry percussion caps.

Bayonets and Scabbards   The bayonet was an important part of the Confederate infantryman's equipment—not just for close-quarter fighting, which did not happen very often, but for entrenching, cooking and any number of other purposes. They were stored in black leather or canvas scabbards, in either the Gaylord or Enfield Pattern.

Canteens   Confederate troops carried a variety of canteens, many of them the wooden Gardner Pattern. There were also metal ones, such as the Richmond Tin Drum Pattern. Captured Federal canteens came in two main styles—Smoothside, or 1858 Pattern, and Bullseye, or 1862 Pattern. Canteen covers were usually made from whatever odd scraps of material were to hand at the time.

Stonewall brigade reenactors march to the battlefield of McDowall (fought in May 1862). *(Bethanna and Joe Gibson)*

Blacks who accompanied the Stonewall Brigade, usually as officers' servants, sometimes took up arms when the brigade went into battle. *(Bethanna and Joe Gibson)*

Camp servants followed their units through every battle of the Civil War, and some could be seen carrying their own weight in pots, pans, and other impedimenta. *(Battles and Leaders)*

Knapsacks and Haversacks   The full-shoulder knapsack soon became obsolete as the war's hard marches increased and men threw off their heavy packs. In the Confederacy it was first replaced by the slung-haversack, which, as Jefferson Davis observed, "the women could make," and ultimately by men just wrapping belongings in their blanket.

Blanket Rolls   The typical Confederate soldier carried a blanket roll, and if he was lucky would also have an oiled cloth or gum blanket that would help keep him warm and dry at night. Slung across the left shoulder (in order to keep one's firing arm free), other items such as tin plate, cup, diary, Bible, card deck and sewing kit could be packed inside the roll, and might even provide a degree of protection when slung across the chest in battle.

Tents   Although the men of the Stonewall Brigade were issued tents, they did not often have wagons to carry their equipment. Consequently, the troops spent a considerable amount of time without cover, and became very good at improvising shelter. Many captured Union field gun shrouds were pressed into service as makeshift tents.

Muskets and Rifles The soldiers of the Stonewall Brigade were initially issued with muskets and rifles of various makes and calibers. At the start of the war, many of the guns were out of date, such as the .69-caliber smoothbore musket. Some units, such as the Rockbridge Greys, arrived at Harper's Ferry with muskets borrowed from VMI. These were smoothbored M1851 Springfield Cadet muskets of .57 caliber. When the Shenandoah Sharpshooters were formed into Company K, 33rd Virginia, they were issued with old flintlock muskets that had been converted to percussion.

Cartridges were made of paper and contained both powder and bullet—they were either tied shut with string or carefully folded over. The guns were all muzzle loaded—the cartridge had to be torn open with the teeth, and the powder poured down the barrel. The bullet was then rammed down the bore with a ramrod, and a percussion cap fitted at the breech. The hammer was then cocked, and when the trigger was pulled the hammer hit the percussion cap, firing the gun. Trained soldiers could fire three shots a minute. Each soldier was expected to carry forty rounds of ammunition in his cartridge box, with an equivalent amount of caps.

The muskets issued to many of the early Confederate soldiers did not have the range of the rifles used by Union troops. In the early part of the war, Federal pickets could fire at their opposite numbers, comfortable in the knowledge that their opponents could not reach them back. It was not long, however, before the Confederates captured enough Union rifles to even the score. In addition, British imports began to arrive in the Confederacy by the end of 1861, and by 1863 enough .577 caliber Enfield rifles had made it through the naval blockade to be issued to the troops of the Stonewall Brigade.

While operating out of Harper's Ferry in May 1861, Jackson posted men of the brigade along the Baltimore and Ohio to execute his plan of capturing the railroad's locomotives and sending them into the Confederacy. *(Century Magazine)*

Near Winchester, Virginia, a squad of skirmishers from the Stonewall Brigade brush against a heavy concentration of Union sharpshooters hidden in the woods near a farmhouse. *(Century Magazine)*

PEOPLE

A year after graduating from West Point, 2nd Lieutenant Thomas Jonathan Jackson fought with distinction in the Mexican War, where he earned two brevets as an artilleryman. *(USAMHI)*

Mary Anna Jackson spent her last days with her husband near Fredericksburg after he was wounded at Chancellorsville. *(Historic Lexington Foundation, Stonewall Jackson House)*

Thomas Jonathan "Stonewall" Jackson

Stonewall Jackson was one of the great commanders in military history. Eccentric, ascetic, demanding and fearless, he was one of those rare individuals who, even in a conflict involving millions, could stamp his own personality on the outcome of events, achieving victory for his cause against daunting odds.

Born on January 21, 1824 in Clarksburg, (now West) Virginia, Jackson endured a rough childhood. His Scots-Irish father died of typhoid when he was two, as did a sister, and his mother died five years later. Along with a surviving sister, Jackson went to live with a strict uncle, helping with farmwork while teaching himself to read and write in his spare time. His older brother, Warren, who had gone to live with other relatives, died in 1841. The next year Jackson's fortunes improved when he was appointed to the U.S. Military Academy at West Point. He initially struggled with the curriculum, but with hard work and discipline improved steadily, finally finishing 17th out of 59 cadets in the class of 1846.

Jackson then served with the 1st U.S. Artillery in the Mexican War, finishing as a brevet major after a conspicuous display of bravery in the assault on Chapultepec. In 1851 he accepted a teaching position at the Virginia Military Institute in Lexington, Virginia. It was here that Jackson joined the Presbyterian Church, becoming a deacon of the congregation. Two years later he married Elinor "Ellie" Junkin, whose father was the head of Washington College; however, personal misfortunes did not cease. Ellie died while attempting to deliver the couple's first child, which was stillborn. In 1857, Jackson married Mary Anna Morrison, whose father would become head of Davidson College, but tragedy struck again when their firstborn, a daughter, died. A second daughter, Julia Laura Jackson (named for his mother and sister) was born in 1862.

As a teacher of the rather incongruous subjects of Philosophy and Artillery at VMI, Jackson was frequently ridiculed by his students, who called him "Old Blue Light," for the flash in his eyes, or "Tom Fool."

Sandie Pendleton, A.A.G.

J. G. Morrison, A.D.C.

D. B. Bridgeford
Provost Marshal

Henry Kyd Douglas, A.A.G.

James Power Smith, A.D.C.

Dr. Hunter McGuire,
Medical Director

Jedediah Hotchkiss,
Topographical Engineering

Wells J. Hawks,
Chief of Staff

Robert Lewis Dabney,
Assistant Chief of Staff

W. Allan
Chief of Ordnance

Stonewall Jackson
Corps Commander

Jackson was extremely strict, seemingly humorless, and would tend to recite his lectures from memory, not accepting questions or discussion. A number of his cadets would serve under him during the war, however, where they would come to idolize him.

When Virginia seceded from the Union, Jackson was appointed colonel and ordered to take command of the volunteers and militia units then assembling from throughout the Shenendoah Valley. He

When appointed lieutenant general and placed in command of the Army of Northern Virginia's Second Corps, Jackson formed his staff around many of the officers who had served in the Stonewall Brigade.

This fellow had the honor of portraying General Jackson in a reenactment. One trusts that there are lemons in his saddlebag. *(Bethanna and Joe Gibson)*

formed the men into five regiments which collectively became the 1st Brigade, Army of the Shenandoah. Accordingly, Jackson was promoted to brigadier general that June.

The following month he rose to fame at the first great battle of the war, Bull Run (or Manassas), where his brigade stood fast before a seemingly irresistible Union assault. It then counterattacked to help drive the Federals from the field while suffering nearly 500 casualties. It was there that he and his brigade received the nickname "Stonewall," a word that would soon resonate through both the North and the South.

Promoted to major general and assigned to command the Shenendoah Valley District, Jackson endured a rough winter of 1861–62. But then came his Valley Campaign in the spring, a series of interconnected battles still studied in the world's military schools as a masterpiece of strategy and tactics. With a command never exceeding 17,000 men, Jackson marched and countermarched 400 miles, defeating three separate Union armies. The result was not only to retain the greater part of the Shenendoah for the Confederacy, but to tie up 60,000 Federal troops, preventing them from joining the Union's larger effort, then underway against Richmond. Instead, it was Jackson and his men who slipped away to join the confrontation on the Peninsula, providing Robert E. Lee the additional strength he required for victory.

Though Jackson had become famous he was still considered eccentric, with a number of odd personal ticks. Convinced that one of his arms was shorter than the other, he had a habit of raising one arm

Commanders of the Stonewall Brigade

Brigadier General Thomas J. Jackson   Apr 27–Oct 28, 1861
    Wounded Chancellorsville, 1863, died Guinea Station, 1863

Brigadier General Richard B. Garnett   Nov 14, 1861–Mar 25, 1862
    Killed in action, Gettysburg, 1863

Brigadier General Charles S. Winder   Mar 25–Aug 9, 1862
    Killed in action, Cedar Run, 1862

Colonel William Baylor   Aug 9–30, 1862
    Killed in action, Second Manassas, 1862

Lieutenant Colonel Andrew J. Grigsby   Aug 30–Nov 6, 1862

Brigadier General Elisha F. Paxton   Nov 6, 1862–May 3, 1863
    Killed in action, Chancellorsville, 1863

Brigadier General James A. Walker   May 14, 1863–May 12, 1864
    Died 1901

Brigadier General William Terry
    Commanded surviving members of the Stonewall Brigade after their
    consolidation into Terry's Brigade. Died 1888

to even them out. He had a belief in the therapeutic power of lemons, though his men never knew where he got them. He hated to fight on Sundays, a fact that may have influenced his campaigns; and he was extremely taciturn, capable of staring at a campfire for hours without saying a word.

The fact that he never divulged his thinking even to his senior subordinates ruffled some feathers during the war. When Richard Ewell first arrived in the Valley only to find Jackson had left him no exact orders, he blurted to an officer: "I tell you, sir, he is crazy as a March hare." Richard Taylor wrote of Jackson: "If silence be golden, he was a 'bonanza.' He sucked lemons, ate hard-tack, and drank water, and praying and fighting appeared to be his idea of the 'whole duty of man.'"

During the Seven Days' Battles in 1862, Jackson turned in his only sub-par performance of the war, a fact disguised at the time by McClellan's retreat and the Rebel public's relief at the salvation of Richmond. But as Lee had seen, the Army of the Potomac could have been crushed during that campaign, especially given Jackson's presence above the Federals' left rear. For three full days, as the Federals turned their backs toward the James River, Jackson failed to put his full force in motion. The reason may have been clinical exhaustion immediately following the Valley Campaign; one observer saw Jackson fall asleep while eating, a bite of food still in his mouth. Others speculated that his religious scruples intervened, since one of the crucial days was a Sunday.

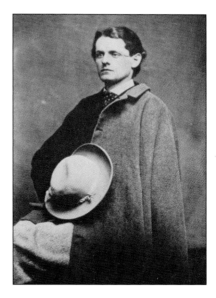

Henry Kyd Douglas spent most of his early life living across the Potomac River from Shepherdstown, Virginia. When the then Colonel Jackson organized the brigade at Harper's Ferry, Douglas signed on as a private in Company B, 2nd Virginia. Douglas eventually became a major and the brigade's assistant adjutant-general. *(USAMHI)*

Whatever the cause, the strange lethargy that seized Jackson on the Peninsula had never been seen before, and during the following year of monumental battles would not be seen again.

Those battles came in quick succession from August 1862 until his death nine months later. Jackson once again employed fast marching, incisive strategic sense, and the indomitable courage of his troops to best a succession of Union generals. During this period, as he worked in tandem with Lee and Longstreet, the Army of Northern Virginia achieved its greatest victories.

During the Second Bull Run campaign, Jackson won the battle of Cedar Mountain, captured and destroyed Union General Pope's main supply base, and then stood alone at Manassas with his corps—not evading battle but initiating it against Pope's entire army. It is difficult to imagine any other corps commander utilizing an isolated position in the enemy's rear to such advantage. Pope's big mistake, in fact, was adhering to the conventional wisdom that Jackson would retreat before superior numbers. Instead, Stonewall stood fast until Longstreet had come up, and it was Pope who was thus demolished.

During the Antietam campaign, Jackson undertook a hard march to attack Harper's Ferry, capturing the equivalent of two Union divisions. The next day he marched to Sharpsburg, where he held the left as Lee's vastly outnumbered army fought the Federals to a standstill in American history's bloodiest day. Thereafter promoted to lieutenant general, at Fredericksburg Jackson held the Confederate right in another repulse of the Army of the Potomac. This victory was only unsatisfactory to the Confederates because the Federals retreated before they had a chance to deliver another crushing blow.

Confederate dead in the "Bloody Lane" at Antietam. Of the 250 men in the Stonewall Brigade that day—the bloodiest in American history—88 were killed or wounded. *(Century Magazine)*

Jackson's value lay not only in his battlefield successes but in the strict discipline he imparted to his command, calling upon his men for superhuman exertions to gain advantage over the enemy. He once said that he preferred his men to drip sweat rather than blood, and his soldiers became known as "Jackson's Foot Cavalry." Between hard fighting, hard marching and utter confidence in their strict commander, Jackson's men assumed an aura of invincibility in both their own eyes and those of their enemies. Late in the war, Confederate Brigadier General Alexander Lawton described the Stonewall he had known:

> He was the true type of all great soldiers . . . His soldiers obeyed him to the death . . . Their respect he commanded . . . Any man is proud to have been one of the famous Stonewall brigade. But, be sure, it was bitter hard work to keep up with him as all know who ever served under him. He gave his orders rapidly and distinctly and rode away, never allowing answer or remonstrance. It was, "Look there—see that place—take it!" When you failed you were apt to be put under arrest. When you reported the place taken, he only said, "Good!"

The apex of Jackson's military career came on the day of his death, at Chancellorsville. The Confederates were outnumbered more than two to one, with Longstreet away. It was left to Lee and Jackson to devise a plan whereby Stonewall would take over half the army and disappear for a day, circling the Federals to reach their vulnerable rear. Such a maneuver was tried many times during the war with poor results: the flanking force would turn too soon or arrive too late, or be detected en route, whereupon it would run into prepared resistance. But Jackson executed the maneuver perfectly with three divisions, giving the Confederacy its most spectacular victory. With the Army of the Potomac in retreat once again, Lee's strategic options broadened, so that one more triumph, perhaps on Northern soil, could win for the Confederacy on the battlefield what the increasingly heavy factors of Union demography and industrial might would otherwise deny her.

It was on that night of May 2, 1863 at Chancellorsville, however, that Jackson was struck down accidentally by his own men. Despite the best medical care the Confederates could provide, he died on May 10 after his left arm had been amputated, from complications with pneumonia. He was given a massive state funeral service in Richmond, where business was suspended for the day, and his body was then taken to Lexington for burial. There was much disgruntlement in the Stonewall Brigade that they were not allowed to attend the services or to accompany their honored commander's remains.

It was Lee who refused the brigade's request, as he felt that every man, including himself, was still needed at the front. Nevertheless it was

Cadet John F. Neff of the Virginia Military Institute had been one of Jackson's students. Elected colonel of the 33rd Virginia in April 1862, Neff was killed on August 28, 1862, while fighting the Iron Brigade at Brawner's Farm. *(USAMHI)*

Lost ambrotypes found in Richmond, Virginia, after the close of the war depict two views of Confederate soldiers as they looked before the battles began. *(Battles and Leaders)*

Lee who mourned Jackson's death more than anyone, describing it as losing his "right arm." Given Lee's style of command, which relied on suggestion and "cordial cooperation" as much as on firm orders, the decisive, self-reliant Jackson had been a perfect subordinate. In the campaigns to come, particularly the one about to be launched into Pennsylvania, the absence of Stonewall Jackson would be severely felt.

The Battle of Gettysburg in July 1863 is often considered to be the turning point of the Civil War, when the Army of the Potomac finally bested the Army of Northern Virginia. But the true turning point might have come on the day seven weeks earlier when Jackson died. Prior to that day the South had been able to glimpse clearly its ultimate goal of national independence; afterward, despite a number of grim defensive successes, the Confederacy's days were clearly numbered. In a letter to John Bell Hood on May 21, 1863, Robert E. Lee wrote:

> I grieve much over the death of General Jackson—for our sakes, not for his. He is happy and at peace. But his spirit lives with us, and I hope it will raise up many Jacksons in our ranks. We must all do more than formerly. We must endeavor to follow the unselfish, devoted, intrepid course he pursued, and we shall be strengthtened rather than weakened by his loss.

Naturally, Lee needed to put the best face on matters, not allowing his or the army's confidence to ebb. An alternative view came from the Confederate diarist Mary Chesnut, after another six months saw continual setbacks for the Confederacy. As she contemplated the fearsome year of 1864, during which Union strength would continue to grow while the Confederacy's ability to resist grew weaker, with ever-diminishing hopes of turning the tables, she reflected the thoughts of thousands of other Southerners. She wrote in her diary on New Year's Day, 1864: "One more year of Stonewall would have saved us."

Richard Brooke Garnett

Born on November 21, 1817, in Essex County, Virginia, Richard "Dick" Garnett graduated from West Point in 1841, fought against the Seminoles in Florida and served as a staff officer in New Orleans during the Mexican War. He was afterward assigned to the Great Plains where he briefly commanded Fort Laramie in Sioux territory.

When the Civil War broke out, Garnett made his way back to the east and served with Cobb's Georgia Legion. In November 1861, he was appointed commander of the Stonewall Brigade after Jackson had been promoted to major general. To the men of the brigade, Garnett's considerate nature provided a stark contrast with the stern demands of Jackson. During the ill-fated march to Romney in January 1862, Jackson and Garnett had words over how hard to push the men. Jackson apparently had a sense that the discipline he had instilled in the brigade had begun to slip under its soft-hearted new commander.

Matters came to a head at the Battle of Kernstown that March, when Jackson misjudged the opposing Union force and the Stonewall Brigade was forced to stand against overwhelming numbers. With his men running out of ammunition and Yankee infantry about to outflank him, Garnett ordered a withdrawal. Jackson, who had been about to bring up reinforcements, was furious, and a week later put Garnett under arrest for "neglect of duty."

The officers and men of the brigade were in turn angry at Jackson, not just because they thought Garnett had acted wisely, but because they thought Jackson had mistakenly thrust them into a one-sided fight. Robert E. Lee released Garnett from arrest and assigned him to temporary command of the injured George Pickett's brigade. Garnett performed well at Antietam and Fredericksburg, and his appointment was made permanent after Pickett was promoted to division command. Oddly enough, he did not resent Jackson personally, and when he was seen to shed tears at Stonewall's casket in Richmond, he was invited to be among the select group of pallbearers.

Less than two months later, on July 3, 1863, Garnett prepared to lead his brigade as part of Pickett's charge on the final day of the Battle of Gettysburg. His leg had been injured and he was so ill that he was forced to wear an overcoat on that hot summer's day. Since he could hardly walk, he rode his horse in the charge, making himself one of the most prominent targets on the field. He was last seen just twenty yards from the Union lines on Cemetery Ridge. His body was never identified, and the Confederates only knew he was dead when his riderless horse limped back to Seminary Ridge. His successor, Colonel Eppa Hunton, said: "He was one of the noblest and bravest men I ever knew."

Hard-drinking and sharp-tongued Lieutenant General Jubal Early assumed command of the Army of Northern Virginia's Second Corps on May 29, 1864, and in June moved it, along with the remnants of the Stonewall Brigade, from the Shenandoah Valley to the outskirts of Washington, DC. (*Battles and Leaders*)

The ordeal at Bloody Angle shattered the Stonewall Brigade, leaving it with fewer than 200 members, no commander—Brigadier General "Stonewall Jim" Walker had been wounded—and only two of its five regimental officers. (*Battles and Leaders*)

Brigadier General Charles S. Winder took command of the Stonewall Brigade during the Shenandoah Valley campaign. He fought on the Peninsula and afterward took command of Jackson's old division. On August 9, 1862, Winder lost his life during the battle with General Banks' corps at Cedar Mountain. *(USAMHI)*

Charles Sidney Winder

Born on October 7, 1829, in Talbot County, Maryland, Winder was part of a wealthy family whose relatives included Francis Scott Key as well as Admiral Franklin Buchanan of the Confederate Navy. After graduation from West Point in 1850 he was assigned to the Pacific Northwest, where he participated in campaigns against the Spokane Indians.

After secession he became colonel of the 6th South Carolina, and took part in the bombardment of Fort Sumter. In April 1862 he was appointed commander of the Stonewall Brigade after Jackson summarily relieved Dick Garnett. Jackson pointedly passed over the five regimental colonels in the brigade, perhaps because they had all vocally stood up for Garnett. To the rank and file, Winder was additionally unwelcome because he was a Marylander, not a native of the Shenendoah Valley from which the brigade drew almost all its men.

Under Winder, however, the Stonewall Brigade saw many of its greatest battlefield successes. Though strict and imperious in manner, Winder was also brave, energetic and a cool-headed commander. At Port Republic his horse was shot three times, yet he continued to rally the line. He also served well on the Peninsula, and Jackson appreciated the stern discipline he applied on forced marches. In between campaigns, however, Winder's harshness, involving various humiliating punishments for straggling or other infractions, prompted even Jackson to object, and caused ongoing hostility among the men.

At the Battle of Cedar Mountain in August 1862, Winder was struck down by a Federal shell while directing the fire of a section of the Rockbridge Artillery. As his mangled body was being carried to the rear, where he would die an hour later, few men showed sympathy. Jackson and other officers, however, mourned his loss. Winder's remains were returned to Maryland where he was buried near his family's home in Easton.

William Smith Hanger Baylor

Born on April 7, 1831, in Augusta County, Virginia, Baylor attended Washington College and studied law at the University of Virginia. In the run-up to the war he was elected an officer of a militia unit, which became part of the 5th Virginia Infantry. During the organization of volunteer units at Harper's Ferry, Jackson described him as his most dependable and deserving subordinate.

Though he lacked formal military training, Baylor was courageous and inspirational in battle, and in April 1862 was elected colonel of the 5th Virginia. He went on to distinguish himself throughout the Valley Campaign, notably at First Winchester. During the Seven Days' Battles he was cited for bravery at Gaines' Mill and Malvern Hill.

After Winder's death at Cedar Mountain, the officers of the Stonewall Brigade petitioned Richmond that Colonel Baylor be promoted as his replacement. They wanted one of their own as commander, not another outsider, and felt Baylor deserved the honor. "The brigade has never asked anything," they wrote, "but we think it has done enough to entitle it to this consideration." Jackson also agreed.

Less than two weeks later, Baylor commanded the Stonewall Brigade in its brutal, stand-up fight against the Union's Iron Brigade. At the Second Battle of Bull Run that followed, Federal troops broke through the Confederate line just in front of Baylor's position. The Stonewall Brigade counterattacked, and after three tries sent the Yankees reeling. During the fight, Baylor grabbed the fallen standard of the 33rd Virginia and called on his men to follow him. He was shot dead seconds later.

Though Baylor's tenure in command was short, terminating before he had even received confirmation of his promotion, the Stonewall Brigade did not have a more valiant commander. His body was returned to Augusta County and was buried in a Presbyterian churchyard.

William S. H. Baylor brought the Augusta Guards, a Virginia militia company, to Harper's Ferry in 1861. During the reorganization of the Stonewall Brigade in mid-April 1862, he assumed command of the 5th Virginia and fell four months later during Second Bull Run. *(USAMHI)*

Andrew Jackson Grigsby

Born on November 2, 1819, in Rockbridge County, Virginia, Grigsby was never officially named commander of the Stonewall Brigade, yet he led it through the crucible of Antietam, and was one of the unit's most colorful figures.

Grigsby flunked out of West Point after earning an appointment in 1837, but then distinguished himself during the Mexican War as a volunteer with the Virginia troops. He settled down to farming in the Shenendoah, but when Virginia seceded he was among the first volunteers to join the new colors. He was appointed major of the 27th Virginia Infantry in June 1861, and the following month displayed his fiery manner of command at Bull Run. He took over full command of the regiment the following March after Kernstown.

Grigsby was an old coot by Civil War standards (five years older than Jackson) but was a soldier's soldier, impatient of protocol and eternally cussing. At Port Republic, while his 27th Virginia stood under a torrent of Yankee fire, his horse was not only killed but fell on top of him. Grigsby turned the air blue with oaths until he was finally able to "dig out" and resume his attack. On the Peninsula he took a ball in the arm, and when one of his men asked if it hurt, he replied, "Yes, damn it. It was put there to hurt!"

The 27th did not perform well at Cedar Mountain while Grigsby was disabled, but after Baylor was killed at Second Bull Run he found himself senior officer of the brigade. At Antietam, Grigsby led the few remaining Stonewallers with indomitable courage. During that blood-soaked day, Grigsby found himself not only leading the brigade but its entire division.

It thus came as a shock in November 1862 when Jackson refused to nominate Grigsby for promotion to official command of the brigade, instead recommending a nondescript member of his staff, Elisha F. Paxton. It has been assumed ever since that Jackson objected to Grigsby's constant use of profanity, while he thought Paxton would have a better moral influence on the men. Once again, the Stonewall Brigade and all its colonels were outraged, and protested the decision about their new commander. Grigsby himself did not take it sitting down and vowed, "As soon as the war ends, I will challenge Jackson to a duel."

He took his argument even farther, in fact, to Jefferson Davis in Richmond. After listening to Grigsby's profanity-laced tirade, Davis finally rose to his feet and said, "Do you know who I am? I am president of the Confederacy!" Grigsby also rose to his feet and replied: "Do you know who I am? I am Andrew Jackson Grigsby of Rockbridge County, Virginia, late colonel of the bloody 27th Virginia of the Stonewall Brigade, and as good a man as you or anyone else, by God!"

Later, 40 officers of the brigade petitioned on behalf of Grigsby, saying, "No bolder or more daring officer ever led troops into a fight or managed them better when actually engaged." But by now Grigsby had alienated all his superiors and had no choice but to resign his commission. He returned home to Lexington where he stayed involved in the cause by training militia units. Ironically, he lived to a ripe old age, dying on December 23, 1895, of natural causes.

Elisha Franklin Paxton

Born on March 4, 1828, in Rockbridge County, Virginia, Elisha "Frank" Paxton was educated at Washington College, Yale and the University of Virginia, going on to become an accomplished lawyer. A problem with his eyesight, however, led him to become a gentleman farmer until war broke out, when he was named a first lieutenant in the 27th Virginia Infantry.

At Bull Run in July 1861 he displayed exceptional gallantry, noted by Jackson, when he picked up a wounded color bearer's flag and helped to steady his regiment. In October Paxton was promoted major of the 27th with hopes of becoming colonel. But he was rejected by the rank and file during the regimental elections of the following spring, the men of the 27th opting instead for A. J. Grigsby. Paxton then volunteered to serve on Jackson's staff. Jackson considered him an extremely valuable officer, and as fellow Presbyterians the two men may also have established a personal bond. When it came time, after Antietam, to nominate a new commander of the Stonewall Brigade, Jackson recommended Paxton.

In April 1861, Elisha Franklin Paxton joined the 4th Virginia at Harper's Ferry and later became a major in the 27th Virginia. After serving as adjutant-general and chief of staff for Jackson's division, Paxton became a brigadier general. He led the Stonewall Brigade at Fredericksburg and was killed on May 3, 1863, near Chancellorsville. *(USAMHI)*

He assumed command in November 1862, much to the consternation of the men. Paxton himself didn't want the job, as he had been perfectly happy on Jackson's staff. Further he felt himself inadequate to the task, and in letters to his wife wrote sad descriptions of the lack of food, clothing and equipment for his men, as well as the terrible casualties they had suffered.

He nevertheless led the brigade well at Fredericksburg, and during the winter of 1862–63 he abetted a religious revival in the camps, arranging to build a chapel that Stonewall himself frequently visited. The men gradually warmed to him, and on the eve of their next great battle, at Chancellorsville, followed him with confidence. On the night of May 2, after the great Confederate flank attack had succeeded, Paxton had a premonition of his own death on the morrow.

When the brigade went into action the next day, Paxton was struck down early in the fight with a bullet through his heart. He was buried in Lexington Cemetery, near Jackson's own grave. The men of the Stonewall Brigade named their next bivouac "Camp Paxton."

James Alexander Walker

Born on August 27, 1832, in Augusta County, Virginia, Walker attended the Virginia Military Institute from where, in 1852, he was expelled for insubordination—in Jackson's class. (It is said that Walker challenged Jackson to a duel.) Afterward he became a lawyer until the outbreak of war, when he was made captain of the Pulaski Guards, which became Company C of the 4th Virginia Infantry. He was then transferred to the 13th Virginia in A. P. Hill's division, where he was steadily promoted until achieving the rank of colonel. After Frank Paxton's death (and Jackson's) at Chancellorsville, Walker was promoted to brigadier general and named as the commander of the Stonewall Brigade.

In April 1861, James Alexander Walker became an officer in Company C, 4th Virginia, at Harper's Ferry. He later transferred to Ambrose P. Hill's brigade as colonel of the 13th Virginia. On May 19, 1863, after commanding Jubal Early's brigade, Walker returned to his roots and led the Stonewall Brigade at Gettysburg, the Wilderness, and Spotsylvania, after which he became a division commander. *(USAMHI)*

Walker led the brigade through the Gettysburg campaign and the beginning of Grant's Overland campaign, earning the nickname "Stonewall Jim." Unlike his predecessor, Paxton, Walker enjoyed a good drink, and it is possible that the brigade's discipline, if not its fighting prowess, slipped during his watch. In the Bloody Angle at Spotsylvania, Walker fought hard to rally his men until taking a shot in the elbow that disabled him for the war.

Once the conflict had ended Walker resumed his law practice and entered politics, becoming a lieutenant governor of Virginia and a two-term Congressman. As late as 1899, when he was 67 years old, he challenged a political opponent to a duel, which he lost, along with the use of his remaining good arm. He lived until 1901, as the last surviving commander of the Stonewall Brigade, whereupon he was buried in Wyetheville Cemetery after a well-attended service.

William Terry became a 1st lieutenant in the 4th Virginia during the brigade's organization in April 1861. He fought in all the major battles and assumed full command of the 4th Virginia at Fredericksburg. Promoted to brigadier general, Terry commanded the Stonewall Brigade at Cold Harbor and remained in command until suffering a wound at Fort Stedman in 1865. (USAMHI)

Confederate horse-drawn artillery moves into position at the Dunker Church, during a reenactment on the battlefield of Antietam. (Bethanna and Joe Gibson)

William Terry

Born on August 4, 1824, in Amherst County, Virginia, Terry graduated from the University of Virginia in 1848 and began his civilian career as a lawyer. After secession he started the war as a lieutenant in the 4th Virginia Infantry, and in 1862 was promoted to major. He distinguished himself on the Peninsula and was wounded at Second Bull Run, returning in time to take part in the battles of Fredericksburg and Chancellorsville, where he was acting commander of the 4th. In September 1863, following Gettysburg, he was promoted to full colonel in command of the regiment.

Terry was never named commander of the Stonewall Brigade, but after the carnage at Spotsylvania (where he was again wounded) he was more or less the last officer standing and so took command of its remnant, along with other decimated Virginia brigades. The combination of the shattered units was called Terry's Brigade, as it performed well as part of Gordon's division under Early, and subsequently during the last stages of the war at Petersburg and Appomattox.

Terry himself was wounded at the Battle of Third Winchester, and finally once more during the charge on Fort Stedman at Petersburg. He was convalescing at home in Wytheville when he heard of Lee's surrender and immediately mounted his horse to try to join Joe Johnston's remaining Confederate army, before his family dissuaded him. After the war he served two terms in Congress and then retired to his farm. He died in 1888 while trying to ford a swollen creek and was buried with full honors in Wytheville, survived by seven children.

ASSESSMENT

During the Civil War, the Stonewall Brigade well earned its reputation as one of the elite units in American military history. In fact, historians have since compared it to famous formations around the world such as Caesar's Tenth Legion, Napoleon's Old Guard or Alexander's Companion Cavalry. The key for the Stonewall Brigade was that, while formed, trained and nurtured by Thomas J. Jackson, it continued to be a primary instrument of his military brilliance even after he had gone on to higher command. It thus took part in nearly every great victory for the Confederacy while its original commander still lived.

It may not be a coincidence that Jackson and his initial command—then called the First Brigade of the Army of the Shenendoah—rose to prominence in the first great battle of the war, Bull Run. No other Southern brigade had been hand-molded by such a unique commander, and its performance on Henry House Hill was no more or less than Jackson had expected.

During the swirl of campaigns and battles that followed in 1862, the men of the Stonewall Brigade played a prominent role in the aggressive fights and grueling marches that typified Jackson's campaigns. Jackson did not always put them in the forefront of his battles, but what he did count on them for was unfailing service at the crucial moment of his operations, whether they initiated attacks or were held in reserve. This confidence that he could reside in his personally trained troops contributed largely to his unbroken string of battlefield successes.

The Stonewall Brigade suffered heavily throughout the war. It lost more men than any comparable unit at First Bull Run, and even more during the battles in the Valley. Through Gaines' Mill, Malvern Hill and Cedar Mountain the brigade continued to shed both men and officers. At Brawner's Farm (Groveton) on the eve of Second Bull Run, when Jackson pitted his old Brigade against the Union's Iron Brigade, they lost 340 men in one of the toughest fights of the war; they lost even more in the two weeks afterward, until at Antietam Creek the brigade was a mere skeleton of its former self with 250 men remaining in the ranks.

In camp along the Rappahannock River in 1863, hungry Confederates try unsuccessfully to catch a rabbit flushed from its burrow beneath a fallen log.

But the Stonewall Brigade had a mysterious way of replenishing itself after hard campaigns. Its men were drawn almost exclusively from the Shenendoah Valley, which, as a major avenue of operations for the Confederacy, afforded the men easy access to their homes, families and neighbors. While this factor helped to maintain the brigade's morale, especially as the Confederates repeatedly reclaimed the Valley, it also contributed to higher desertion rates than were present in other CSA formations. For example, at the Battle of Fredericksburg, the first major clash after Antietam, the ranks of the Stonewall Brigade had grown again five-fold, as stragglers and other tired warriors resumed their stations.

The brigade's culminating moment came at Chancellorsville in May 1863, when the Army of Northern Virginia won its most spectacular victory. But at that battle the brigade lost its third straight commander killed in action, and Stonewall himself was mortally wounded. It was a tragic incident of friendly fire, though Jackson remained conscious for several days and did not expire until he had received a report of his old brigade's stellar performance.

After Jackson's death, the Stonewall Brigade no longer remained a primary instrument of strategic victory for the Confederacy. In fact, there were no more spectacular victories, as the balance in Lee's army shifted to Longstreet's First Corps, even as the Union steadily gathered its inherent numerical and industrial superiority. Beginning with

Gettysburg, less than two months after Chancellorsville, the Federals would not only begin to take advantage of their superior numbers but also the sudden lack of coordinaton, or perhaps brilliance, on the part of Confederate commanders.

At Gettysburg, in a corps now led by Richard Ewell, the Stonewall Brigade played a subsidiary role while the primary fighting was done by Longstreet's corps. The same was true nearly ten months later in the Wilderness, when the Stonewall Brigade held fast on the Confederate left, but was not involved in the crucial actions that decided the battle on the right. It was barely a week later, at Spotsylvania, when the brigade was all but destroyed while trying to hold the Bloody Angle against a surprise Union attack that Lee did not anticipate.

Reduced to less than the size of a normal regiment, and merged into a consolidated brigade of Virginians, it is noteworthy that the few remaining men of Jackson's original command never dropped their collective identity as the Stonewall Brigade. This was difficult to recognize on any battlefield during the last few months of the war. But memories saw farther than tactical commanders on the field, especially among the Confederates. After Lee finally surrendered the Army of Northern Virginia on April 9, 1865, one small unit was requested to lead the ceremonial procession in front of the respectfully onlooking Federal troops.

It was the remnant of the Stonewall Brigade that was asked to lead the Army of Northern Virginia in its last few minutes, just as it had so gallantly led the army in prior days, when the aspirations of the Confederacy were still vibrantly alive.

General Robert E. Lee, commander of the Army of Northern Virginia from June 1, 1862, until the last day of its existence, on April 9, 1865. *(Library of Congress)*

Confederate prisoners captured at Gettysburg. *(Library of Congress)*

REFERENCE

Lost Victories, a thought-provoking analysis of Stonewall Jackson and his campaigns.

Alexander, Bevin, *Lost Victories: The Military Genius of Stonewall Jackson*, New York: Henry Holt, 1992.

Contains an excellent overview of Jackson's campaigns, within the controversial thesis that Stonewall possessed a more astute sense of the Confederacy's strategic possibilities than Lee.

Alexander, Edward Porter, *Fighting for the Confederacy* (originally published *ca.* 1880, G. W. Gallagher, ed.), Chapel Hill: University of North Carolina Press, 1989.

Perhaps the most frankly analytical of all Confederates memoirs, the author having been privy to high command but unburdened by its failures. As Longstreet's artillery chief, Porter did his own job well enough.

Casler, John O., *Four Years in the Stonewall Brigade* (originally published 1893, revised 1906), Columbia: University of South Carolina Press, 2005.

One of the most fascinating memoirs by a Civil War private ever written. From Casler we learn not only of heroic participation in battles but of the mechanics of straggling, looting and robbing the pockets of the fallen. If one has ever read the angelic "Company Aitch" one should also read Casler, in order to discover Samuel Watkins' evil twin.

Catton, Bruce, *The Civil War* (2 vols.), American Heritage Publishing, 1960.

First published for the Civil War centennial, this pictorial work still holds up nearly 50 years later, with analysis that has not yet been surpassed.

Douglas, Henry Kyd, *I Rode with Stonewall*, Chapel Hill: University of North Carolina Press, 1940.

An essential memoir, full of insights, by one of Jackson's aides.

Hattaway, Herman, and Archer Jones, *How the North Won: A Military History of the Civil War*, Urbana: University of Illinois Press, 1983.

A groundbreaking work that boiled the Civil War down to science. The book's casual command of facts, amid its cold-eyed strategic analyses, can strike the reader as irrefutable.

Hennessy, John J., *Return to Bull Run: The Campaign and Battle of Second Manassas*, New York: Simon & Schuster, 1993.

A terrific, detailed account of the often underestimated campaign against the Union's short-lived Army of Virginia.

Henry, Robert Selph, *The Story of the Confederacy* (originally published 1931), New York: Da Capo Press, 1989.

The "lost cause" antidote to Hattaway and Jones (above). In Henry's telling the Gettysburg campaign was by no means a mere "raid," as the principal hopes of the South rested upon Lee's success.

Johnston, Joseph E., *Narrative of Military Operations During the Civil War* (originally published 1874), New York: Da Capo Press, 1990.

Mainly a quarrelsome tome; but Johnston is very detailed and his descriptions of the war's first year are essential.

Long, A. L., *Memoirs of Robert E. Lee: His Military and Personal History* (originally published 1886), New York: Blue and Grey Press, 1983.

Not a memoir of Lee but of his military secretary who observed him closely throughout the war.

Long, E. B., *The Civil War Day by Day: An Almanac 1861–1865*, New York: Doubleday, 1971.

The best and most detailed Civil War book of this kind. The current work, for example when encountering disparate casualty figures, relied on Long for the final verdict.

Longstreet, James, *From Manassas to Appomattox* (originally published 1896), New York: Da Capo Press, 1992.

Whatever one may say about Longstreet and his rather strange, though detailed, memoir, he observed Jackson closely and had firm opinions of his own about the Confederacy's best strategic options. The trick to this book is reading in between the lines.

Paxton, E. Franklin, *Memoir and Memorials: Elisha Franklin Paxton, Brigadier-General, C.S.A.*, New York: De Vinne Press, 1905.

A moving posthumous portrait of Paxton, drawn largely from letters he wrote to his wife.

Robertson, James I., Jr., *The Stonewall Brigade*, Baton Rouge: Louisiana State University Press, 1963.

The best and most detailed book on the Stonewall Brigade from its beginning to its end, covering all its important battles and commanders.

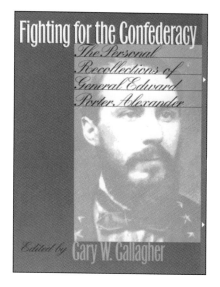

No one had a sharper eye for detail throughout the war than Porter Alexander.

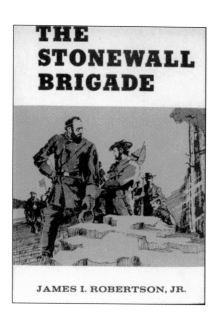

Robertson's *Stonewall Brigade* is a thorough and exciting read by a masterful historian.

"Old Pete's" memoir can be just as enigmatic as the man himself.

Sears, Stephen W., *To the Gates of Richmond: The Peninsula Campaign*, New York: Tickner and Fields, 1992.

An exemplary work on the Seven Days' Battles, not sparing Jackson for his lack of initiative during that crucial week when Lee commanded the largest Confederate army of the war.

Selby, John, *The Stonewall Brigade*, Oxford, UK: Osprey, 1971.

A fine short work, marked by detailed original illustrations and insightful descriptions of Confederate uniforms as they really appeared.

Taylor, Richard: *Destruction and Reconstruction: Personal Experiences of the Late War* (originally published 1879), Nashville: J. S. Sanders, 1998.

An eloquent memoir with vivid descriptions of the Valley Campaign, in which Taylor's Louisianians played a major role.

Wert, Jeffry D., *A Brotherhood of Valor: The Common Soldiers of the Stonewall Brigade, C.S.A. and the Iron Brigade, U.S.A.*, New York: Simon and Schuster, 1999.

An ambitious work juxtaposing the two most famous Civil War brigades in the east, which succeeds brilliantly in terms of both action and detail.

Woodword, C. Vann, ed., *Mary Chesnut's Civil War*, New Haven: Yale University Press, 1981.

A female socialite's diary of the war, written after encountering nearly every significant Confederate commander in her parlor. An important work for describing the true sense of the Southern public.

Other Sources

The War of the Rebellion: A Compilation of the Official Records of the Union and Confederate Armies (70 vols.), U.S. Government Printing Office, 1880–1901.

Commonly called the Official Records, this author relied on the scanned version on Cornell University's "Making of America" website.

Battles and Leaders of the Civil War (4 vols.), the Century Company.

Compiled beginning in 1883 by the editors of *Century* magazine, this four-volume work, drawing on surviving commanders from both North and South, is an essential resource for frank—at times argumentative—accounts of nearly every battle of the war.

North and South, The Official Magazine of the Civil War Society.

The best Civil War magazine in terms of in-depth analysis, frequently featuring debates among historians. A regular highlight is Al Nofi's monthly "Knapsack" column on aspects of everyday life during the war.

Every issue of *North and South* is eagerly awaited.

Internet Sites

www.civilwarhome.com   Created and run by Dick ("Shotgun") Weeks, simply the best Civil War site on the web, expanding with new info all the time.

www.stonewall.hut.ru   A superb site on Jackson and his campaigns, curiously dedicated to "all the Russians" who died in the Civil War.

www.stonewallbrigade.com   Run by one of America's top CW reenactment groups, or "living history associations," with photos, descriptions and analysis.

www.docsouth.unc.edu   Documenting the American South, created by the Univ. of North Carolina at Chapel Hill, contains a wealth of primary material.

www.nps.gov   The National Park Service site, with details, maps and photos of many battlefields.

www.civilwar.org   Run by the Civil War Preservation Trust, contains photos and info on battlefields, particularly those in danger of disappearing.

www.historynet.com   Run by the Weider History Magazines Group, contains many good articles on the Civil War as well as other conflicts.

ABOVE: The front page of the Civil War Preservation Trust website.

BELOW LEFT: Part of the National Park Service website on Gettysburg.

BELOW: Richmond's Museum of the Confederacy (www.moc.org) has a wide range of Civil War exhibits.

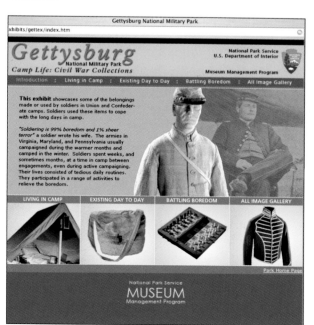

INDEX